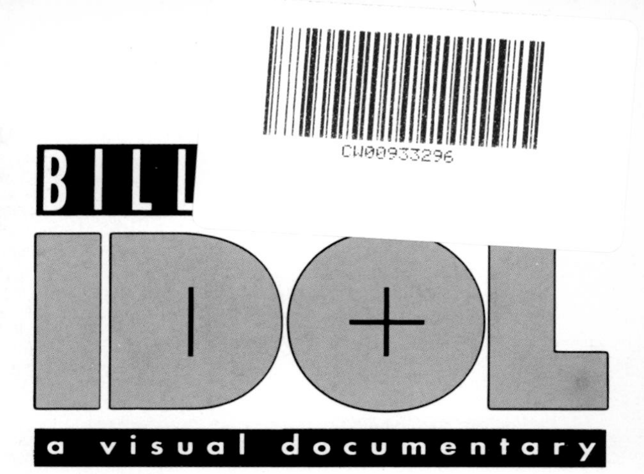

BILLY IDOL

a visual documentary

MIKE WRENN

OMNIBUS PRESS
LONDON · NEW YORK · SYDNEY

Edited by **Chris Charlesworth**
Cover designed by **Robert Fairclough/ Four Corners**
Book designed by **Peter Dolton**
Design and production in association with **Book Production Consultants, 47 Norfolk Street, Cambridge**
Picture research by **Paul Giblin** and **Dave Brolan**
Typesetting and co-ordination by **Caroline Watson**

ISBN 0.7119.2399.X
Order No. OP 46101

Exclusive distributors:

Book Sales Limited,
8/9 Frith Street,
London W1V 5TZ, UK.

Music Sales Corporation,
225 Park Avenue South,
New York, NY 10003, USA.

Music Sales Pty Ltd.,
120 Rothschild Avenue,
Rosebery, NSW 2018, Australia.

To the Music Trade only:
Music Sales Limited,
8/9 Frith Street,
London W1V 5TZ, UK.

Picture credits:
All pictures London Features International except:
All Action 83C
Andre Csillag 74, 78, 79BL
Steve Granitz 38
Pictorial Press 3, 24, 26, 30T, 33, 35B, 49, 51, 65B, 66T, 66B, 75, 79TR
Barry Plummer 14, 20, 21T, 21B, 22T, 22B, 23T, 23B, 80, 82R, 83L, 83R, 87B, 90T, 92
Relay Photos Limited 17, 18T, 50T+B, 57, 67
Retna 28, 62, 93B

Typeset by **Cambridge Photosetting Services**
Printed by **Ebenezer Baylis & Son Ltd, Worcester**

Every effort has been made to trace the copyright holders of the photographs in this book but one or two were unreachable. We would be grateful if the photographers concerned would contact us.

Johnny Rotten called him the 'Perry Como of punk', the UK press went on to call him much worse, but Billy Idol has always looked adversity in the face, and triumphed.

Even when the fallen Idol came a cropper – quickly learning what it's *really* like to suffer pins and needles in the leg – he clawed his way back into the saddle, and hurtled back on the road for his most extensive world tour to date.

But it hasn't always been tough at the top for our Billy. It's been tough at the bottom too. Growing up in the wilds of English suburbia, it can't have been easy convincing friend and foe that one day he'd become a world-wide megastar. Indeed, it couldn't have helped when, for his first few years on the ladder, the closest he'd get to fame and fortune would be sharing a squat with Des O'Connor's daughter Karen!

A rebel without applause during his days with Generation X, Billy hit the big time in America thanks to his enterprising videos which became hugely popular on the recently established MTV channel and, consolidating his position with a string of top-selling albums, the singer has since made a name for himself in all corners of the globe – though not always for the right reasons, as you are about to see . . .

"Writing songs in this rock 'n' roll existence of mine, makes me feel like I'm on the edge every day. I like to feel like I'm facing up to things head on. Like when I ride my motorbike. I know I could put it down and kill myself in a second. And I suppose life is like that."

Billy Idol, 1990.

A VISUAL DOCUMENTARY
1955–1974

William Michael Albert Broad is born in Stanmore, Middlesex, on November 30, 1955 – to be brought up a God-fearing, Bible-reading youngster. The only musical background within his family is his Irish grandmother who, Billy later claims, could play 14 musical instruments.

With his father planning a new life for the family in America, Billy moves to Long Island, New York, at the tender age of three.

After four or five years Stateside however, the family Broad move back to south-east England (Bromley, Worthing and Bromley again), where Billy – by now a manic Beatles fan – is incarcerated in the good old English school system.

Billy's best mate at school is Steve Severin, who will later find fame and fortune as guitarist with Siouxsie And The Banshees. In these days though, his name is Bailey and his hair is long, lank and mousey brown – just like Billy's in fact!

Thrown out of the Scouts for, reputedly, snogging a Girl Guide behind the hot dog stand at a church fete, Billy starts to put all his efforts into learning the guitar. His first instrument is a present from his grandad – a plastic one bought from Woolies – but it isn't long before he graduates to the real thing.

Funding his new-found hobby by caddying for his golf-mad father at 50p a round, the pre-peroxided teenager does well enough at school to earn a place at Sussex University, where he goes to study English and Philosophy during the early seventies.

The age of punk is dawning however, and Billy drops out at the end of his first year. Instead, he returns to base in Bromley, and begins to plot his future career in the music business . . .

"I GREW UP in America when I was a little kid. From the age of three until I was seven or eight I lived in Long Island, so I've got a lot of American relatives, a lot of whom are Irish-Americans. So I'm not just sitting here aware of English culture, the Good Humour ice-cream van is quite real to me, and so's the idea of people water-skiing all day. I've grown up with all that, so it means *something to me."*

"WHEN I LIVED in America first time around, the thing I remember mostly is that Elvis was on the radio all the time. And there were huge fins on the cars, and it was all Walt Disney, bright colours and drive-ins. My dad was pursuing the American dream, but he didn't find it, so we came back home."

"SCHOOL SUCKS."

"I TOOK RELIGIOUS instruction at school, so I could get out of slicing-up chloroformed pregnant rats in Biology. I hated Biology . . . We had this really good teacher who taught us what the Bible was really about. I thought, 'Wait a minute, it isn't just some bloke going around spouting off a load of garbage all the time, hey!' There were these zealots, who were like fucking guerrilla rebels who hated Jesus because he was advocating peace! He showed me that the Bible was all about society. It was really exciting, he showed me the wild *side to the Bible!"*

"I NEVER PLAYED in bands or anything when I was at school. That's really boring and stupid. I didn't want to play in lots of bands. Just one – the one that played what I wanted to play."

"WHEN I WAS growing up, I had long hair and round glasses like John Lennon – until about 1973 when we all went into the David Bowie thing. For a second, when my parents saw me cut my hair, they thought I was going normal. But . . ."

"UNIVERSITY WAS TOO like school, too peculiar. Nice people, but not real. They all fell about in horror when I said 'fuck' in the poetry class. Because I had short hair, they all thought I must be in the army."

"AROUND THE EARLY seventies, I went out with this chick who had a brother that loved The Velvet Underground and had all of Iggy's records. And we'd be listening to this stuff like 'Heroin', dealing with the darkest side of life, and I'd think, 'Wow! This is great!'"

"I LOVED THE idea that Lou Reed isn't the greatest singer in the world, but listen to 'Coney Island Baby' and tell me that ain't singing. 'Cos it's his words and his whole attitude that goes along with it. And I thought, that's what's missing. And when I heard Iggy, I thought, this is brilliant – because these guys can't play at all, but they can*! And of course the best thing in the early seventies was playing Iggy's records to everyone, 'cos they hated him!"*

"I *REMEMBER I worked at the Post Office one Christmas, and I was singing to myself, and this guy turned around to me and said, 'Never try to earn a living by singing, man, because you haven't got a voice!'* "

"M*Y FATHER WAS a big influence on me at the time . . . because he hates music. It's great to have someone around who hates what you like. And it really helped me* choose *what I liked, thank God. Because he didn't believe in music, that proved its wealth to me.* "

"T*HAT WAS ANOTHER thing about having really long hair when I was younger . . . It annoyed my father – it was great!* "

"N*O WONDER I went wild when I got back to London – after* Worthing*!* "

"T*HE IDEALS OF punk rock weren't dictated to me. I was sitting there, figuring it out myself – we all were. When I was at university I was just reading a lot, treading water. All I knew was that I wanted to do something that made me happy, that was exciting and good fun. I didn't know what to do. It was wild that all that stuff was just starting then – The Sex Pistols . . . It was great to see that there were other people who just wanted to fuck about with the record companies and not treat it like some important career.* "

A VISUAL DOCUMENTARY 1975

As the punk scene prepares to explode in Britain, Billy's already in with the 'in' crowd, hanging-out with a group of like-minded teenagers in south-east London. Soon to become known as the Bromley Contingent, they're the first, and probably the most *devoted* fans that The Sex Pistols will ever have. Initially despised by McLaren's mob, the 'contingent' are eventually welcomed, with the press picking up on them almost as much as the band.

"TO ME, ROCK 'n' roll was always the great escape. I was one of those kids with no future 'til I got in a rock 'n' roll band – because I didn't want to do the normal thing. I hated the idea of having to work for somebody. So being in a band was really another attempt to get away without working."

"I KNEW THAT I didn't possess any spectacular singing ability. And because of that I always found it difficult to find people to play with – because by the early 1970s everyone was incredibly caught up in the musical side of rock 'n' roll. And in everyone's eyes, I was the least musical person around."

"I WAS BORED with the music that record companies were allowing people to hear. They had a stranglehold on music, and it was through people like Siouxsie, The Sex Pistols and us that it was broken. That's what punk was about – giving people something different, giving them a choice. But I'd never have gotten into it if there'd been enough other people providing that kind of music for me."

"WHEN I WAS *starting out – wanting to get a band together – it was all just rock 'n' roll. It must have been someone on some paper who termed it 'punk rock'. But punk was just rock 'n' roll – just like music is music. And all* we *can do, is play the music* we *want to play.* "

"I ALWAYS LIKED *the idea of having to force people to do things. That's what punk was all about – well if they don't listen, you just go and bang 'em over the head with it! And the great thing was, once me and my friends – people from The Banshees – started to hang out, it was all there right in front of you, right there in SEX – Malcolm McLaren's boutique on the Kings Road – the next fashion, the new this, the fucking next stuff! You'd walk along the road and tell people, 'In two years' time you're all gonna look like this!' And they'd all laugh at you. Then two years later,* they'd *have the spiky hair job as well.* "

"I USED TO *deliver power tools to construction sites (while working for his father's tool-hire company). The Irish workmen hadn't seen a punk rocker before. They thought it was incredibly funny seeing this guy with bleached blond, spiky hair, and 'Sex Pistols' written all over his jeans. They used to just crack up for hours.* "

"PUNK ROCK WAS *a definite 'fuck you', in a lot of ways. But I think, in the end, it happened 'cos we totally believed in it . . . It was all about discovering yourself, rather than everybody discovering you. You discovered yourself, and then foisted it on* them. *I think we were all people who had a lot of potential. We weren't necessarily brilliant musicians, but we found a way around it. And the way around it was punk rock.* "

"Y'KNOW, IT WAS *an old chemistry teacher at school who started it really. He wrote on my report once, 'William is idle.' Me dad went mad, but I hated chemistry anyway so I was quite pleased. I'd been toying with the idea of becoming a musician, and punk was* the *thing in the seventies. It allowed you to do anything you wanted and sod everyone else! I couldn't really call myself by my real name. Bill Broad sounded like a well-hard skinhead – like I was about to boot your head in. Punk was all about changing your name and stuff, so I thought that – thanks to the chemistry teacher – I'd be Billy Idle. For a* larf. *But then I thought, no – I'm not just some bum who sits around on it doing eff-all. So I settled on the other spelling. Idol – it sort of implied that I was some great rock star already, even though I wasn't – and it really* was *taking the piss!* "

"ALL I EVER *wanted to do, was to be as great as I can be.* "

1976

february

Billy tries his hand at song-writing, with the help of another Pistols fan/Bromley contingent member – Susan Dallion, a trainee dental hygienist who's soon to be known world-wide as Siouxsie Sioux . . .

august

Not content to live in The Pistols' shadow forever, Billy decides to start his own band – to be launched soon after the obligatory ad in *Melody Maker*.
Bassist Tony James is the first to respond. Formerly with London SS – a rehearsal room outfit involving Mick Jones (later of The Clash) and Brian James (later of The Damned) – he's desperately looking for a band to actually play some *dates* with.
Together with a singer by the name of Gene October (formerly with Love And Kisses), Billy and Tony agree to form a group called Chelsea. Billy settles for playing guitar, while John Towe is dragged in on drums.

october

Chelsea perform their first live engagement at London's ICA – as support act to Throbbing Gristle.
Chelsea secure a gig backing a stripper named Shelley, performing a set which includes 'Gloria', 'For Your Love', 'Rebel Rebel' and several early Rolling Stones numbers.

december

With Chelsea showing all the potential of their footballing namesakes, Billy and Tony break rank to form a brand new outfit, Generation X – the name being taken from a sixties paperback concerned with those evergreen subjects of sex, drugs and rock 'n' roll. Drummer John Towe also chooses to make the transition and, with Billy switching to lead vocals, the group is finally augmented by guitarist Bob 'Derwood' Andrews.
On December 12, Generation X play *their* first gig – this time at the capital's Central College Of Art And Design.
Deliberately shunning the 'working-class and angry' mould, the band immediately suffer from a credibility problem as far as the mainstream press are concerned. But with early gigs going down well, they are quick to gain favour with the people that matter – the paying public. Indeed, so immediate is their popularity on the live circuit, that *Sniffin' Glue* fanzine finds itself compelled to explain the phenomenon. "Generation X care about melody and arrangement," the editorial exclaims. "They sing songs about a new way of life." A new way of life it may be, but dressing it up in sixties riffs and target T-shirts does little to impress the serious-minded record companies, who continue to give the boys a wide berth.

"*WE WERE TIRED of listening to the old rockers, so we became our own entertainment.* "

"*IT'S TRUE . . . SIOUXSIE and I did try to write some songs together, but they weren't any good.* "

"*AROUND THE TIME I was hanging out with the people who ended up in Siouxsie And The Banshees – and the other punk bands – I was listening to Iggy, but at the same time to stuff like Frank Zappa, The Mahavishnu Orchestra, and things like that. But it was obvious to me that Iggy was the total answer, because I couldn't be John McLaughlin to save me fuckin' life! I didn't want to stand around communing with nature!* "

"*THEN I HEARD The Ramones' first record, and I thought that was fuckin' brilliant. We got that first record, and every song was under two minutes, and it was like a revolution. People now probably don't realise it – because it was such a long time ago – just exactly what that record did. But we were playing normal speed until we heard The Ramones, and because of them, we revved everything up. Everybody did, because The Ramones really had their groove, and we were all still searching for ours. The Clash, us, everybody. The Ramones were like the next step.* "

"*THE SEX PISTOLS were singing 'no future', and there* was *no future aside from what we were doing. It's funny, but we were creating our own future, and that was the exciting thing. You didn't live for tomorrow. You really did say, 'Fuck, it's right now that counts.' Even the whole thing of Billy Idol – I started off with I-D-L-E, and then thought, 'We're kings in our own right'.* "

"*MY DAD GAVE me hell when I told him I wanted to be in a rock 'n' roll band.* "

"*WHEN WE FIRST started Generation X, we were just tooling around London. We were just doing it. I mean, we weren't even thinking about recording contracts. Obviously we were writing songs and making music together, and we were obviously thinking that one day we're going to make a record. Whether we made it or not, didn't matter. That's what was so great about it. We had this innate belief that what we were doing was worthwhile, no matter what happened. And of course when it did get big, it just made us think how right we were. But that wasn't the goal.* "

"*PEOPLE WERE CRANKING out songs every five minutes. The Clash would come over with their new one, we'd play them* our *new one – The Sex Pistols would play* their *new one . . .* "

"*MY ON-STAGE 'image' isn't really made up. When the music hits me, that's me feeling spontaneous. I become that person you see on-stage. I've always been the same. Even in Generation X, I had me fist in the air, 'Whooo! C'mon!' . . . It's not something that's put on. It's part of me. And that's just part of punk rock, what we believed in. You have to go in there and take people to the pits of hell, you have to, to give it that spark and make it more exciting. It's what we wanted to be like, and it's what* I am *like.* "

1977

january

billy and the boys play a set at the opening of a brand new punk venue, The Roxy.
John Towe leaves Generation X, to be replaced by Mark Laff, formerly of Subway Sect. The gigging continues . . .

march

Desperate to attract the attention of a major label, Generation X spend the next few months in and out of the studio, laying down demos and completing a series of cuts including 'Your Generation', 'Day By Day', 'Change Our World', 'Youth Youth Youth', 'Gimme Some Truth', 'From The Heart', 'No No No', 'Rockers', 'Endless Dreams Of Billy Idol' and 'Love Like Fire'. These *original* recordings would later emerge in June 1987 on a collection labelled 'Original Generation X', to be put out by McDonald Bros Records.

april

Generation X step in at the last minute to replace The Clash as support to John Cale at London's Roundhouse.

july

Following the phenomenal success of a session they do for John Peel's Radio One spot, Generation X at last sign a deal with Chrysalis Records.

september

The band's début single is finally unleashed. Entitled 'Your Generation', the call-to-arms comes a little late in the decade for most critics, and the record is widely ignored. Significantly though, it still manages to reach 36 in the UK chart.

december

With the punk movement now visibly suffocating in a cloak of congealed gob, Generation X release a follow-up single, 'Wild Youth'. Like its predecessor it contains all the natural ingredients of a classic punk anthem. But *again*, it arrives at least six months too late.

" *IT WAS ALL a massive joke to us – y'know, playing The Roxy and having all these record company people giving us their cards.* "

" *YOU KNOW, HOTEL windows are so boring. I once took out all the ones in my room. I simply wasn't in a very good mood, I suppose.* "

" *WE THOUGHT WE were the total antithesis of Led Zeppelin, Foreigner and Journey.* "

" *IT SEEMS LIKE yesterday – but it* is *a long time ago. I'm still feeling and looking the same, doing the same kind of thing. Generation X were just a punk rock 'n' roll band – our influences were The Who, MC5, The Stooges – I was writing melodies but it was still punk rock in intent. I'm not a musician, we weren't professionals. The whole point at the time was* not *to have loads of copies of The Sex Pistols. So we were different. The Clash were different. It was very hard for me to pretend to be all nasty and dirty and horrible. That's why I was Billy Idol. I wasn't rotten* or *evil.* "

" *WE WERE JUST a load of silly twats, really. We weren't a punk group, we were a punk* rock 'n' roll *group, because we always loved rock 'n' roll and we didn't mind saying it. But neither the press nor the record company understood any of that. Actually, I don't remember all that much about those days. But it's all dotted about in there, the old punk memories I suppose. Playing the Roundhouse when The Clash wouldn't play – that was the biggest stage we'd played on, and the worst gig! The Lyceum when the audience just threw things at me for the whole of the gig, and I just exhorted them to throw things because I didn't give a damn. I don't miss much about any of that.* "

1978

march

A new single, 'Ready Steady Go', is released as a trail-blazer for the forthcoming album. It makes it to 47 in the singles chart. The band's long-awaited début LP finally reaches the shops. Simply titled 'Generation X', it peaks fairly impressively at 29 in the UK chart. Produced by Martin Rushent, the album would later be made available on CD. Tracks are: 'From The Heart'/'One Hundred Punks'/'Listen'/'Ready Steady Go'/'Kleenex'/'Promises Promises'/'Day By Day'/'The Invisible Man'/'Kiss Me Deadly'/'Too Personal'/'Youth Youth Youth'.
A 25-night, nationwide tour is launched . . .

december

'King Rocker' (a tribute to Elvis Presley) emerges as the lads' seasonal offering, and becomes their biggest seller to date – finally making it to number 11 in the Christmas countdown, following an appearance on *Top Of The Pops*. Entertaining as the song is however, much of its success must be put down to the mainstream marketing ploy which accompanies its arrival. Four alternative picture sleeves are made available, each corresponding to a different member of the band, and *each* containing different coloured vinyl! The Tony James version is pink, Mark Laff's is yellow, Derwood's is orange, and Billy Idol's is . . . blood red! Well, what else?

"*I DON'T KNOW what I was doing with my voice (on that first album). It sounds like I was emasculated! At the time it didn't sound too bad on the little stereo speakers we were listening back on in the garage. And it didn't sound too bad with the phone ringing and poor old Martin Rushent trying to mix us, The Stranglers, run the United Artists A&R department* and *do 999 all at the same time. Yeah, it sounds okay, but there's no power.*"

"*SEX IS THE best way of spending a night.*"

"*ROSES GET YOU everywhere . . .*"

"*I THINK THE weirdest sex I ever had was with this chick in San Francisco, on a Generation X promotional tour. The girl was a stripper who lived with this other girl – who she was always making it with. When we got back to my hotel she said to me, 'Make a fist.' It was all pretty exciting and wild, because I hadn't done that before. But the problem was, she came for about an hour. Then she said, 'Well that's it.' And I thought, 'Thank God for that,' because I didn't know if I could hold out much longer . . . Then my hand blew up like a balloon. I couldn't walk around with my hand all blown up, because I had all these interviews to do the next day. So I phoned down to room service, got a bucket of ice, and fell asleep with my hand on the ice. When I woke up the next morning my hand was back down to normal. That was one of my first introductions to America.*"

A VISUAL DOCUMENTARY

1979

january

Generation X's new album, 'Valley Of The Dolls', is released. Tracks are: 'Running With The Boss Sound'/'Night Of The Cadillacs'/'Paradise West'/'Friday's Angels'/'King Rocker'/'Valley Of The Dolls'/'English Dream'/'Love Like Fire'/'The Prime Of Kenny Silvers (Parts One And Two)'.

Produced by former Mott The Hoople star, Ian Hunter, the record is flavoured with the essence of glam-rock and, needless to say, receives a serious slagging from most areas of the press. Generation X are seen to be dressing-up, both their music *and* themselves, at a time when serious social climbers are all dressing-down. And with trench-coated critics pandering to trench-coated sounds, Billy and the boys find good cause to worry about their future. The LP peaks at 51 in the UK, and the writing already appears to be on the wall.

february

The title track from 'Valley Of The Dolls' is chosen as a single. Put out in brown vinyl this month, and black vinyl the next, the song finally climbs to 23 in the chart.

june

'Friday's Angels' is given a spin as the next '45', first on pink vinyl, then on black. The record staggers to 62, and the dumper beckons ever closer.

september

News breaks of dissatisfaction in the ranks, where Mark Laff and Bob Andrews are said to be unhappy with the aims and ambitions of the principal pairing. In consequence they both decide to leave during the ensuing weeks, the former eventually re-emerging as a founder member of Twenty Flight Rockers, with the latter going on to minor success with Westworld.

With things at an all-time low for Billy and Tony, no-one is too surprised when news surfaces of a long-running litigation battle with manager Stuart Joseph.

"BY THE TIME Generation X put out the second album, we had become quite distant. The whole thing had just drifted and I found myself beginning to pander to young people's ideas about what they wanted us to do. I didn't get into music to start pandering to other people. The whole thing behind punk was getting to do what you wanted."

"'VALLEY OF THE Dolls' was a disgusting display . . . Ian Hunter produced the LP. He's a nice guy and he did his best, but we really didn't apply ourselves to it. It's easy to make excuses, but I won't – it's just a bad album."

"THE FIRST ALBUM was the only great stuff, and all that was written when we were in Chelsea – me doing the music, Tony the lyrics. I didn't like 'Valley Of The Dolls' at all . . . 'King Rocker' was alright. If I do the old songs now, I try not to change them – but do 'em just the same. I always hated it when people like The Who used to jazz up old songs."

"EVERYTHING ABOUT GENERATION X was fantastic until around the time of 'Valley Of The Dolls', and then things inside the group started to crumble . . ."

"WE HAD PROBLEMS with our manager, who was basically a rip-off merchant, but it took us a year to agree to do something about him – and then a further 18 months with the lawyers to get rid of him, by which time Generation X were virtually forgotten. That's when the first band finished."

"PEOPLE HERE LIKE music to be pigeon-holed. Y'know, they tried to dump Deep Purple and Pink Floyd together as progressive bands, but they were nothing like each other."

"THERE WAS A guy from Sheffield who came to all our gigs and knew every word to every song, and he was standing in the middle of all these punks with 'Status Quo' on his back. The trouble we had at our gigs wasn't with the HM kids fighting the punks because they didn't like the same stuff – but with punks fighting with skins 'cos they *didn't like anything!"*

"AFTER 'VALLEY OF The Dolls' I sat down with Generation X and told them if they didn't do this 'Dancing With Myself'/'White Wedding' music, I was going to leave the group!"

1980

january

Deciding to stick with it, Billy and Tony recruit the original Clash drummer, Terry Chimes, but fail in their attempts to secure a suitable guitarist. Instead, they vote to continue as a three-piece for the moment, using a selection of stand-ins (notably John McGeogh and Steve Jones) during a frantic series of recording sessions for the third album.

september

With a 'permanent' guitarist – James Stevenson – finally, and ironically poached from Chelsea, the band re-emerge with a new single, 'Dancing With Myself', and a new name . . . Gen X. The trick doesn't work however, and the single once again stalls at 62 in the UK.

december

Gen X set up their final series of live dates . . .

"*TONY AND I did a third album, but the group were just friends – they weren't the basis for a new band. That's why we called ourselves Gen X for the last album.*"

"*IT TOOK ME ages to get Terry Chimes' number. I got it off Mick Jones in the end. He'd got it written on the corner of his Gran's wall or something . . .*"

"*TONY AND ME weren't writing together as we used to – so I just thought it was the right time to knock it on the head.*"

"*EVERYTHING GOT SO bad with the band . . . it was just as if things were out to destroy me! It was really heavy, there was a lot of betrayal when Generation X ended. It was all very weird. Now I understand a lot more about things, I realise that life is just like that. But then it was a fight for survival . . .*"

"I KIND OF knew that the band was going to split up, after we did that little tour in December. The group just wasn't playing any good. I felt we just weren't giving the fans what they deserved – I know *we weren't. It was the same old Gen X it always was – one night we're on, two nights we're off – and that's not really good enough when you've been playing for five years! I thought it had a lot to do with how we all felt about the music. I remember when we first started, we were really* kicking *on the music – we played good most nights – it might have been a bit lousy on the rhythm end, or I might have sung out of tune, but the* feeling *was there. And some nights that was really missing. It wasn't really a group any more, it really was a put-together thing. It didn't have the feeling that the early Generation X had, it just had this kind of heaviness about it, it had got stodgy. It was a shame because the music we were playing wasn't stodgy, and I don't think it was coming out like that. So that's really why it had to end. I don't think we were giving the people what we were capable of."*

1981

january

The band's third album finally sees daylight. Entitled 'Kiss Me Deadly', its track listing runs: 'Dancing With Myself'/'Untouchables'/'Happy People'/'Heavens Inside'/'Triumph'/'Revenge'/'Stars Look Down'/'What Do You Want'/'Poison'/'Oh Mother'. It's produced by Keith Forsey, former Giorgio Moroder sidekick, and *future* Billy Idol 'controller'.

In an inspired marketing move, 'Dancing With Myself' is re-issued – on *clear* vinyl – with a different B-side. This makes all the difference of course, and the record . . . *a-hem*, rockets to a high of 60 in the UK.

The situation is somewhat different in America however, where the single gives every appearance of being a solo release from Billy Idol. Not unnaturally then, when 'Dancing With Myself' becomes a hit Stateside, Billy finds himself in something of a dilemma. Should he stay with his burned-out band, or should he jump ship to pursue a solo career in America? Silly question really, and one which Billy's new manager – Kiss boss, and brief Gen X adviser Bill Aucoin – seems happy to er, advise on.

As for Tony James, *he* seems determined not to be outdone, and is already making plans to perpetrate one of the biggest hypes the music industry has ever seen. It won't be long before his extraordinary brainchild, Sigue Sigue Sputnik, will become the band on the nation's lips. He's thought of everything – the hair, the make-up, the suits, the shoes, the attitude, even the size of the advance from EMI – in fact, it'll only be the 'music' that lets him down. That and the fact that SSS end up looking like a bunch of psychedelic spring onions . . .

september

'Mony Mony' is released. It's Billy Idol's début single as a solo artist. Perhaps significantly however, the record company doesn't break Billy away from his past *too* abruptly, and actually includes 'Untouchables' and 'Dancing With Myself' on the 12-inch/EP version of the single.

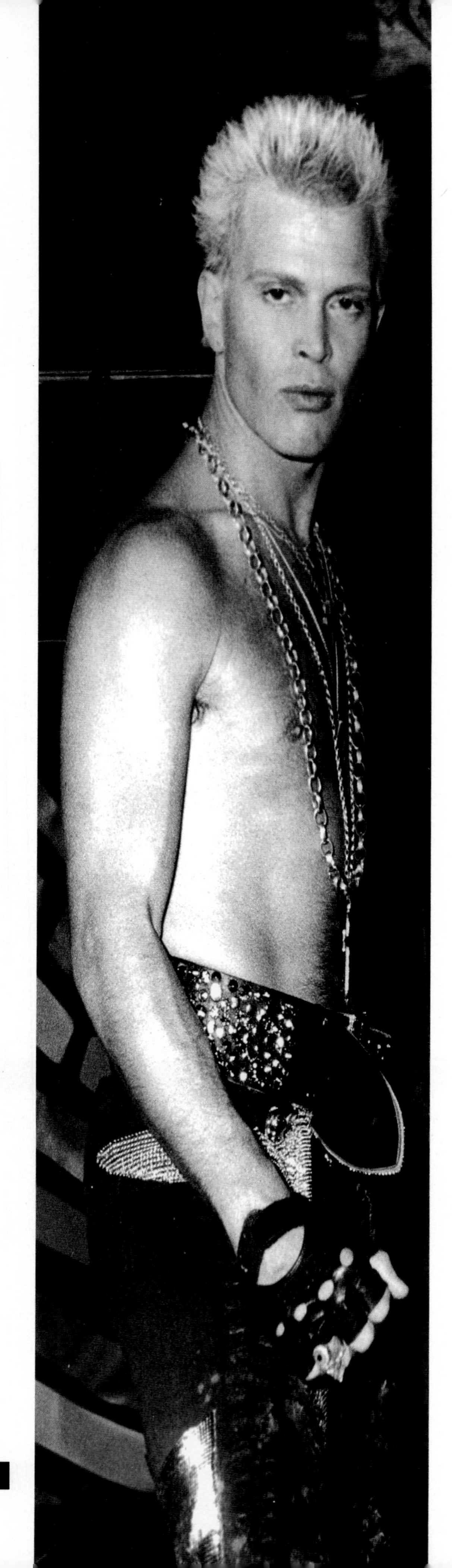

"*EVERYBODY HAD HAD it with me. The fans thought I was trying to be such a big fucking star – and that I was turning my back on them.* "

"*I KNOW EVERYONE thinks I sold the band down the river . . . but I can tell you this – if it wasn't for me, the third Generation X album would never have come out. I told Chrysalis that they had to put it out. I told them we had all worked on it really hard. Terry Chimes had put a year's work into it, and Tony James and me had put* five *years into it, and Keith Forsey had come all the way to do it, and we'd all worked our bollocks off. John McGeoch had come in, and he'd gotten all involved and excited when he could've just been sitting in with The Banshees. We thought it was a valuable piece of music, one way or another. But they didn't want to put it out because they didn't think it would sell. And it did sell, quite good.* "

"*THINGS GOT SO heavy, I had to get out or go nuts. I really went through hell, but I think I needed to in a way. It was the only way I was going to understand and be strong enough to do what I'm doing now – and actually* last *doing it.* "

"*IN ENGLAND, RECORDS come out quicker and are over a lot faster than in the States. It's either up the charts in three weeks, or going nowhere fast. That's why there's a massive turnover in groups there, because the country gobbles them up and spits them out. I never turned my back on punk rock. That initial explosion was over – period. British music seemed too into techno bands and light pop. The audience changed. Rather than be an old has-been, it seemed better to go to where people still saw rock 'n' roll as fresh. I wanted to go on playing energetic music, with real people, and that just wasn't going on in London any more.* "

"*I DESERTED AN England that didn't believe in rock 'n' roll. As far as I can see, all they really wanted was Boy George.* "

"*I WANTED TO mix technology with pure rock 'n' roll. I wanted to get that never-ending beat that drives you wild, whether it's a slow throb or a crazy rock number.* "

"*A LOT OF good groups were coming out of New York – Suicide, Talking Heads – so it seemed a pretty favourable place to be, in terms of finding similar types of people to those I'd knocked about with in London.* "

"*ON THE FIRST Generation X album, Tony James and myself were the main forces within the group. When we came to do the second album, 'Valley Of The Dolls', the other members of the band wanted a lot more say in the music, so we tried to do everything democratically. But* that *meant there was no real focus. And by the time we'd taken the group back – on the last album, 'Kiss Me Deadly' – it was already a bit too late in terms of England. Punk rock had kinda run its course . . . It's great to be democratic, but it's shitty if the music sucks.* "

"*YOU JUST COULDN'T move to our music . . .* "

"PEOPLE REALLY GET hurt easily by things, y'know. Something like Gen X breaking up really fucks them up. They think, 'Oh he's gone off to make lots of money, what a sell-out!' or something like that – and three years later they'll change. And that's kind of what happened with the press before we did that last album. They really hated us for three years, and finally they go . . . all positive . . . And of course it's too late. We'd already blown it, in terms of ourselves. But that's the way things are."

"BILL AUCOIN WAS my manager at the time, and he lived in New York, so I moved there. It seemed so natural because, at that time, New York had so many after-hours clubs. I mean, you could find five different clubs a night, and never go to the same place twice. And it was going to these clubs that I started to realise just how many people liked 'Dancing With Myself'."

"I ALWAYS LOVED the music that came out of New York – The Velvet Underground, The New York Dolls. So when I looked at the scene in England and really thought about it – I could have stayed there but I think in the end, for a lot of people, I would have been a bit of a has-been. 'Dancing With Myself' had been a huge club hit in America, and Generation X never played in the States, so it wasn't like anybody had ever seen us. It was a lot more exciting to be looked upon as something new, as opposed to something that's over. And I wasn't in a position where I could sit back on any laurels. I was still carving out my own destiny and musical style. So it was a really great time for me, in the sense that I was struggling in a place which is always in turmoil."

"I REMEMBER I went to Hurrah one night, and I was just standing at the bar – and the bar was really crowded – and then suddenly the DJ slammed on 'Dancing With Myself' and the whole place jumped up, knocking over everything to get to the dance floor. So I thought, 'I've definitely done the right thing moving to New York'."

"I WANTED TO record 'Mony Mony' because it was the first record I ever made love to."

"MY FIRST YEAR in the States was pure frustration . . . You can't get a good hairspray over there, for love nor money!"

HAMER

1982

january

The record company tries to persuade Billy to alter his image. They soon realise it's a losing battle, and eventually they give up.

february

Billy cements a new working partnership – with guitarist Steve Stevens and producer Keith Forsey – by putting together the finishing touches of a solo LP.

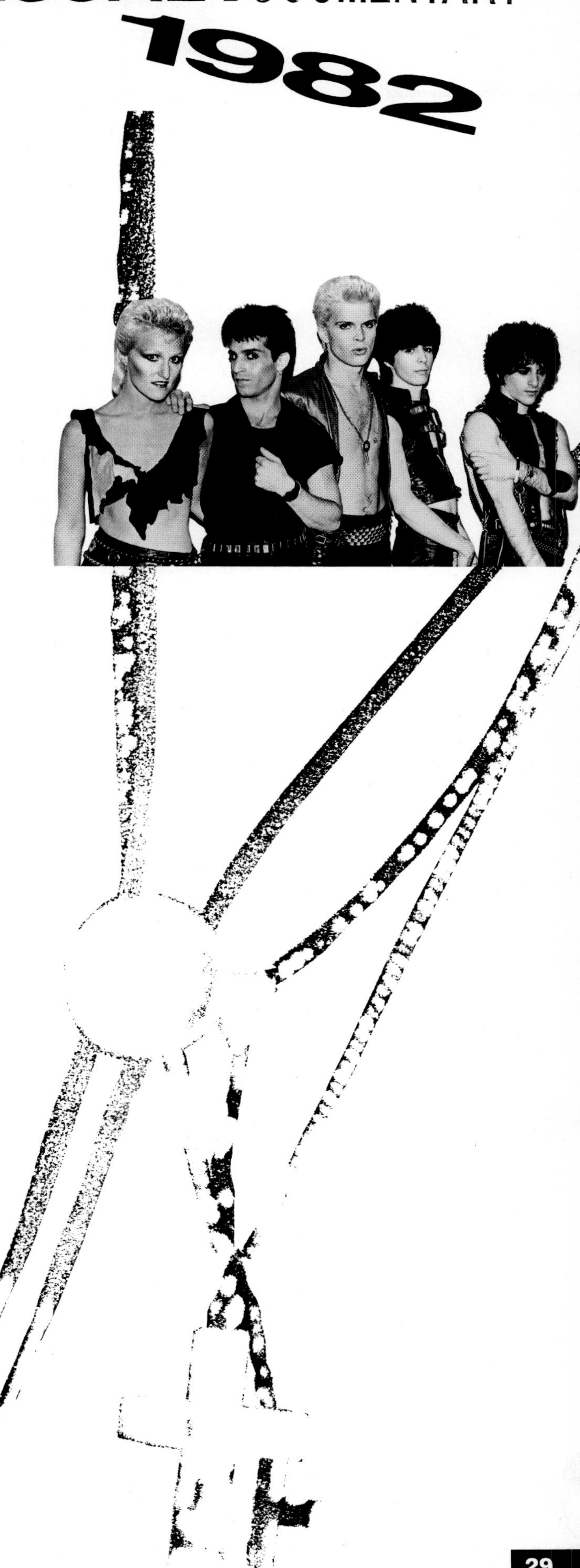

july

Billy's long-awaited début album at last reaches the shops. Eponymously titled, tracks are: 'Come On, Come On'/'White Wedding (Part 1)'/'Hot In The City'/'Dead On Arrival'/ 'Nobody's Business'/'Love Calling'/'Hole In The Wall'/'Shooting Stars'/'It's So Cruel'/ 'Congo Man'.
Note, 'Mony Mony' is not included on the LP.

august

Almost a whole year since the release of his first solo single, the follow-up hits the streets. 'Hot In The City' turns everyone on to the *sound* of Billy Idol but, in his home country at least, few people actually buy the record. In America though, it's a resounding success.

october

The celebrated 'White Wedding' is unleashed for the first time, but Billy will have to wait for its brilliance to be fully recognised at home. In the United States however, the singer's formularised rock 'n' drawl seems to be winning over quite a fan club. The rock video channel MTV clearly plays a major part too – it's already giving a good deal of air-space to his fantasy-torn promos. The one for 'White Wedding' costs Billy £35,000, but then it has been shot by David Mallet (famed for his ground-breaking 'Ashes To Ashes' clip for David Bowie) – which naturally helps attract even more attention from TV producers Stateside.

*"A*T THE START *of 1982, no-one really wanted to know me. I was a has-been – or, if I'm honest, a never-really-was. So I had to prove everyone wrong. I was the* only *person who had any* real *faith in me, or my songs! But I did it. "*

*"T*HE RECORD COMPANY *wanted me to change my name, and change my image. I said, 'What's going on!? I've spent the last five years being Billy Fucking Idol – I'm not gonna change now!' "*

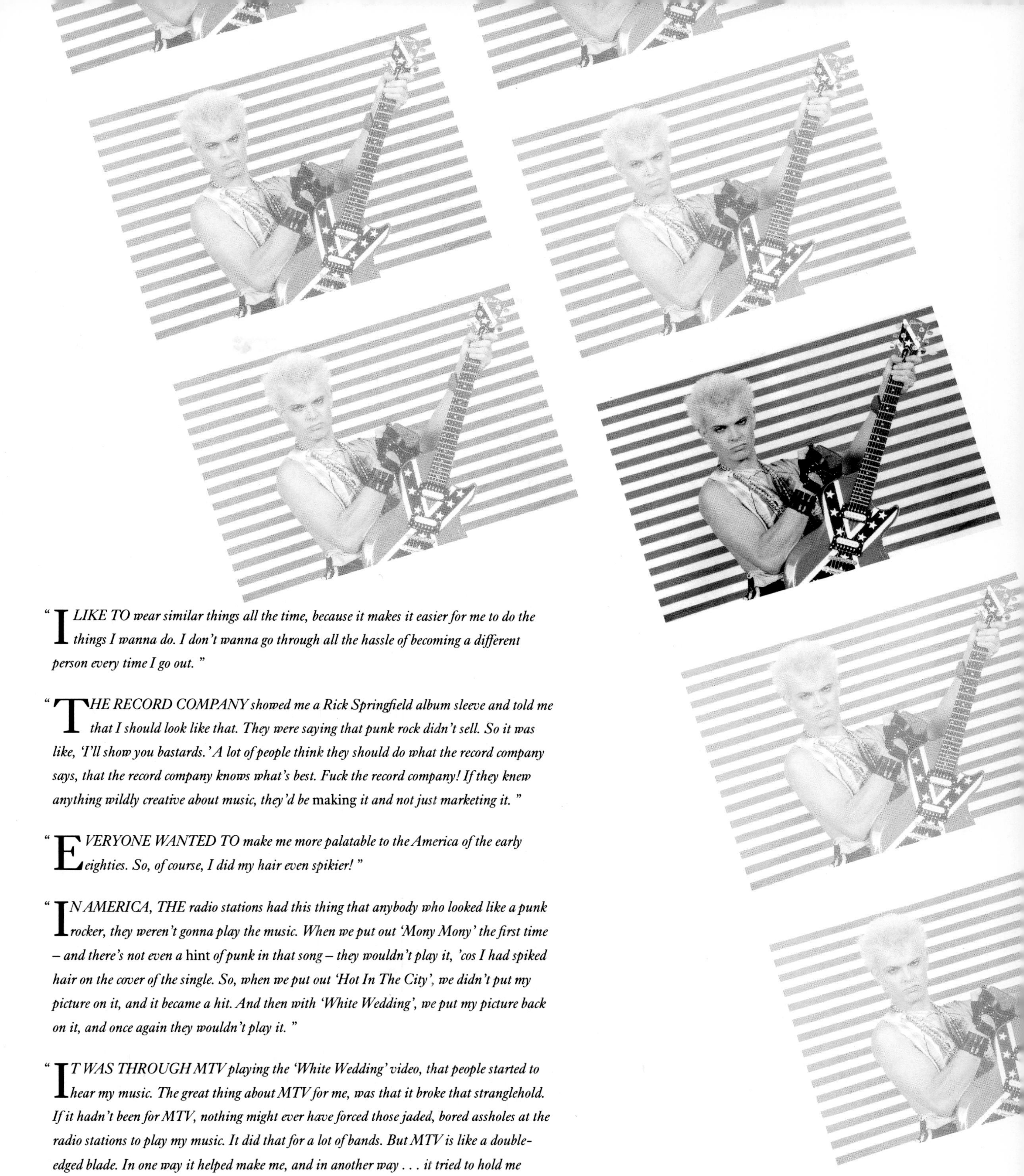

" **I** *LIKE TO wear similar things all the time, because it makes it easier for me to do the things I wanna do. I don't wanna go through all the hassle of becoming a different person every time I go out."*

" **T** *HE RECORD COMPANY showed me a Rick Springfield album sleeve and told me that I should look like that. They were saying that punk rock didn't sell. So it was like, 'I'll show you bastards.' A lot of people think they should do what the record company says, that the record company knows what's best. Fuck the record company! If they knew anything wildly creative about music, they'd be* making *it and not just marketing it."*

" **E** *VERYONE WANTED TO make me more palatable to the America of the early eighties. So, of course, I did my hair even spikier!"*

" **I** *N AMERICA, THE radio stations had this thing that anybody who looked like a punk rocker, they weren't gonna play the music. When we put out 'Mony Mony' the first time – and there's not even a* hint *of punk in that song – they wouldn't play it, 'cos I had spiked hair on the cover of the single. So, when we put out 'Hot In The City', we didn't put my picture on it, and it became a hit. And then with 'White Wedding', we put my picture back on it, and once again they wouldn't play it."*

" **I** *T WAS THROUGH MTV playing the 'White Wedding' video, that people started to hear my music. The great thing about MTV for me, was that it broke that stranglehold. If it hadn't been for MTV, nothing might ever have forced those jaded, bored assholes at the radio stations to play my music. It did that for a lot of bands. But MTV is like a double-edged blade. In one way it helped make me, and in another way . . . it tried to hold me back."*

1983

january

Billy starts the year as he means to continue – by working on a collection of new songs.

september

To prepare fans for Billy's imminent return, Chrysalis re-issue 'White Wedding' and 'Hot In The City' on *one* single. The 12-inch also features 'Love Calling' from the 'Billy Idol' album, and 'Dancing With Myself' – America's favourite Gen X number.

"THE REASON WHY I wrote things like 'White Wedding' and 'Rebel Yell', with that simple rock backbeat, was because that's the way I could control the musicians around me and create something that had my style in it – so nobody could fuck with it. 'Cos that's what people do, they ruin it. If you keep everything simple, then they can't get it wrong."

"I'VE BEEN WRECKED all my life."

"ON A LEVEL where people knew about it, punk rock only really arrived in America in 1983. No-one really told them, or when they did hear about it they heard about the antics *rather than the music. They never played The Pistols on the radio, let alone Generation X. Their biggest problem was being uninformed. I think my being here has helped to inform them a bit. I hope so."*

" *PUNK ROCK* IS *rock 'n' roll. Gene Vincent was a punk rocker, so was Eddie Cochran, so was Elvis, so am I – all relatively ordinary people whose skills or whatever have been built up by ourselves, without help or years in the 'biz'. Punk is to do with a way of thinking. That's why Jim Morrison was a punk, why Iggy Pop and to a certain extent David Bowie is – they are all interested in being autonomous. They don't need to be bolstered up by record companies, managers or anything else.* "

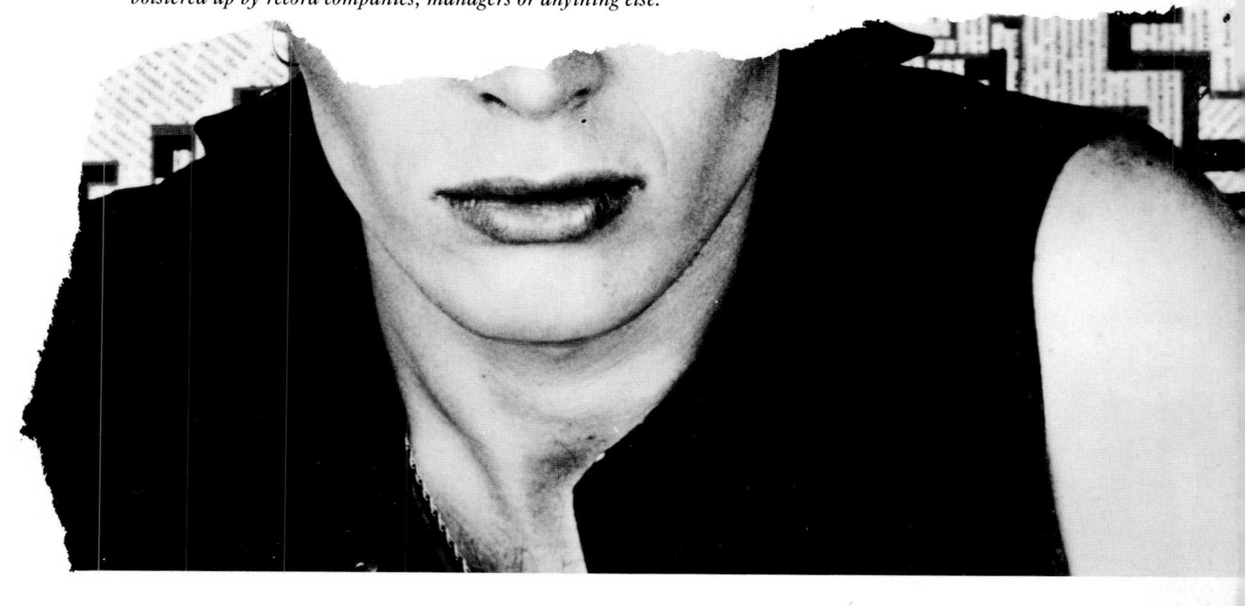

1984

january

Billy launches a busy period by promoting his first *new* single for 16 months – 'Rebel Yell', culled from the album of the same name, which is also released this month. Full track listing reads: 'Rebel Yell'/'Daytime Drama'/'Eyes Without A Face'/'Blue Highway'/'Flesh For Fantasy'/'Catch My Fall'/'Crank Call'/'(Do Not) Stand In The Shadows'/'The Dead Next Door.
The album will later win Idol a Grammy nomination, alongside long-established mega-stars Elton John, David Bowie, Bruce Springsteen and, it says here, John Mellencamp.
The ensuing US tour is a phenomenal success.

june

'Eyes Without A Face' is picked as the next promotional single, and duly does its stuff by bursting into the UK Top 20. Sales are clearly assisted by the inclusion of 'Rebel Yell' and (surprise, surprise) 'Dancing With Myself', which both appear on an extended 12-inch, and which also augment 'Eyes Without A Face' in a special double-packed 'single' presented in a gatefold sleeve. Oh, and they're all included on a picture disc too, of course.

september

'Flesh For Fantasy' is released as a single, and the marketing department surpass themselves with their ingenuity. The 12-inch carries a free poster of Sir William himself! The *song* becomes an instant anthem for strippers the world over . . . I'm reliably informed.

october

Billy gets talked into co-writing his own film script – based on the life and work of Elvis Presley. Entitled *King Death*, the project will never actually materialise on screen, but is destined to take up a good six months of the star's time.

“I DON’T THINK *my music* sounds *American . . . American rock – and I mean all of it, Quiet Riot included – is really bland. But what* I’m *doing doesn’t have the same kind of mix . . . American rock bands like to crowd everything in, drums and guitars and keyboards, all piled one on top of the other. But I’ve gone for a far more expansive sound. I reckon that what I’ve got now is the music that went into ‘Dancing With Myself’, only with a little more finesse. If you listen to Generation X records you can hear what I was doing then and what I’m doing now really isn’t that different.* ”

“*IT’S ALL A question of taste. In 1977 I said I loved Eddie Cochran when it was really unfashionable. In 1978 there was a rockabilly revival and I was suddenly a hero. It’s all a question of style – and timing.* ”

“*I’M NOT PART of the British invasion. My group all come from America, we’re an American group. I don’t believe in this ‘invasion’ anyway. It’s all a media tactic to fight back the rise of black music in this country.* ”

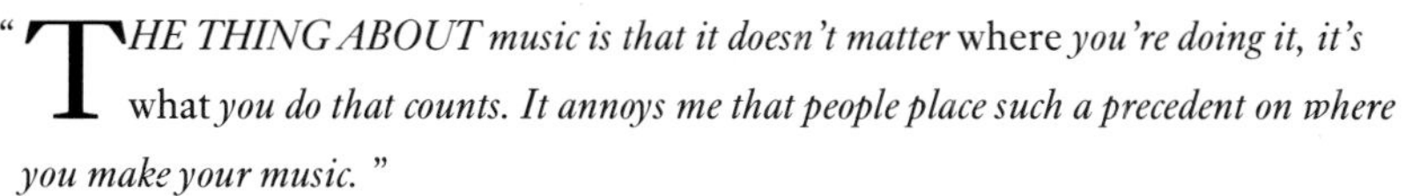

"THE THING ABOUT music is that it doesn't matter where *you're doing it, it's* what *you do that counts. It annoys me that people place such a precedent on where you make your music."*

"ALL THESE 'WHY did you come to America?' questions, all this guff about 'He went to make a lot of money', or 'He's left England' – I've never left England, I just came to live in New York, that's all."

"WHAT THE FUCK'S the point? What does it matter American or English? Didn't we pinch it from them in the first place?! The English have been trying to sound American ever since Johnny Kidd And The Pirates."

"I THINK WHAT'S happening to a lot of groups is that they do these videos . . . but can't always back it up live. I can, because the music is the basis of everything I do. I've been doing it much longer than I've been making silly videos."

"I'M KIND OF getting sick of these people who call me a misogynist. If people are threatened by my image, good. But my songs, and my videos if you look at them, are very supportive of women."

"'REBEL YELL' IS *a song about crying out. Not about punk rebels or anything, but the rebel yell of ordinary people who want to stand up and cry out for more for the poor, more for everybody! I wrote the song originally about women – that they don't want slavery, that they won't sit and beg. There should be a fantastic relationship that's one to one, that's strong enough because of the individuals, that should lead to great sex, not because it's a man and a woman, but because two people are in love. Yet it turns out that the song is just as much about America being my personal rebel yell. I went there at a time when I thought I'd never write another song – and when I thought I'd have to give up – but I found Steve, and I found a home in New York.* "

"MY DAD GAVE *me hell when I wanted to be in a rock 'n' roll band, I want to give* him *hell for the fact that he didn't believe in me. He chose not to talk to me for two years because I had long hair . . . Well, there you are dad, a* million *Americans have bought my record!* "

"WHY AREN'T I *doing so well at home? . . . Because Chrysalis UK hate rock 'n' roll bands. I've been second to someone else all along. Second to Blondie, second to Spandau Ballet, and second to Ultravox!* "

"IF I MADE *pop records – instead of rock 'n' roll – then maybe I'd be huge in Britain too!* "

"THE ENGLISH RECORD *company just didn't believe in me . . . At the time of 'Rebel Yell', I went there to do some promotion, and I was sitting up in the A&R office after everyone had gone home, and I wanted to play a track off 'Rebel Yell'. So I looked around the office, and I couldn't find a 'Rebel Yell' or* any *Billy Idol record anywhere. So I thought,* right! *and I just trashed the place. And I wrote all over the walls, WHY ARE THERE NO 'REBEL YELLS' HERE? I was just so pissed off. It really fucking bugged me. It made me vengeful, and I really wanted to show the English bastards – and stick it up their bum.* "

"THE WEIRDEST THING *about the English chart, is just how poppy it's gone. At least in America there's people like Prince and that. I know that's started to happen here but, a few months back, there was Kajagoogoo, Duran Duran . . . and Wham! I mean, people with suntans and shorts!! I just don't see it . . .* "

"WHEN 'REBEL YELL' *became such a success, a lot of avenues opened up to me. And one of the things that people started to talk to me about was film. I didn't really believe that anyone would be interested in putting money into a film with me as the star. It wasn't even something I wanted to do. But after the tour that year went so well, people in Hollywood kept calling, and the next thing I knew I was flying out to discuss an idea I'd got – based on a book called* King Death. "

"KING DEATH *IS an allegorical story about Elvis Presley and his manager. The film companies really went for it, and I suddenly found myself starring in this film. The writing of the script took over my whole life for six months. Fortunately it never came to fruition. And it really took me away from the music. It took a long time before I could get the music going again. A lot of the initial energy between Steve (Stevens) and myself had dissipated. I think the time spent on the film, without actually getting anywhere, was a bit of a downer."*

"*THERE'S A PARK near where I live in New York, and all the drug dealers who hang out there have named their product after my songs. So you can score 'Rebel Yell' smokes, 'White Wedding' cocaine, and 'Dancing With Myself' quaaludes . . . Fantastic!!!"*

"*SYNTHS ARE ALRIGHT, but there's no* attack *is there? You strap on a guitar, play a chord, and it's right there vibrating your bollocks . . . You'll never get a synth to vibrate your bollocks!"*

"*WHY DO I employ a synth player? . . . Because she looks a million dollars!"*

"*GROUPIES DON'T EXIST . . . They're my friends, and I have sex with them because I like them."*

"*IT'S NO EASIER for me to meet girls than it is for anyone doing any kind of job. Merchant seamen, businessmen, anyone can get as many girls as I do."*

"*IT'S NOT EASY being me. It's hard in this business, but it can be enjoyable. I like it now because I have such a wide audience – though Generation X did too. There weren't enough punks in Britain to buy as many records as we sold, so we must have had lots of other fans too."*

"*MY FANS ARE my friends. We like each other. People used to give me such flak. They'd say, 'How can you be a punk rocker if you care about people?' But that's what punk was all about. We cared enough about people to give them the choice of what they wanted . . . That's what I think now as well. I haven't changed since then. I'm still the same Billy Idol."*

SHERIFF

june

A new story breaks – 'Billy Idol Is Dead' – except he isn't.

Another rumour, this time suggesting Billy has developed a serious drug problem, is not so readily ignored.

Word also has it that Billy has split with both his manager *and* his long-standing girlfriend (the former Hot Gossip dancer) Perri Lister. While the break with Aucoin is to be a permanent one (for the time being he'll be managed by an Englishman who worked for Aucoin, Brendan Bourke, who also manages Debbie Harry) Billy and Perri will fall out a few more times yet before anyone need take *that* one too seriously.

september

A year since the release of his last single, Billy re-emerges with 'To Be A Lover', a Top 30 hit heralding the arrival of a brand new album . . .

'To Be A Lover' (a cover of a Booker T/William Bell composition, which Idol had originally heard on an album by reggae artist George Faith) goes on to be nominated for a Grammy – in the Best Male Rock Vocal category of 1987.

october

The 'Whiplash Smile' album is released, representing his first collection of 'new' songs for two years and nine months! Tracks are: 'World's Forgotten Boy'/'To Be A Lover'/'Soul Standing By'/'Sweet Sixteen'/'Man For All Seasons'/'Don't Need A Gun'/'Beyond Belief'/'Fatal Charm'/'All Summer Single'/'One Night, One Chance'.
Billy lines-up an extensive US tour.

november

Lip Service Records announce the arrival of 'An Interview With Billy Idol' – a conversation hosted by Kris Needs, and starring Sir William himself!

" I'VE BEEN LUCKY, really fucking lucky. I know a lot of this happens because of the way, I think, that I take risks – but I'm such *a lucky bastard. It's hard to live with the idea that people are focusing on your sodding life a bit more than they used to. It's just weird. I've never really had it before, so I'm sort of dealing with it. "*

" I DID *FORGET to be a lover. I was always eager to push everything away to make my dreams come true. When it came to the end of the sessions, what did I do? I recorded my favourite song. It showed me where I wanted to go. It was the last song for that album – and the root of the next one. "*

" I HADN'T PLANNED to use 'To Be A Lover' at all. But I couldn't get it out of my head, so I recorded it anyway. It turned out so well, that it had to be a single. "

" I WENT THROUGH emotional changes in the fact that I split up with the girlfriend I had had for a long time, and was very much in love with. Up to that time, one of the hardest things to do was to write love songs . . . Especially in my case, a lot of people look at me and think that I would be soft if I sang about love, whereas that's one of the most difficult *things to sing about. It's really hard to get your emotions out, and it took until I went through a period of heartbreak to really write about it. I think when you search inside yourself, you are really looking for things that make you happy – and happiness is the hardest thing to sing about. "*

" PEOPLE DO MESS about with you, and do really silly things. You have to tell them to fuck off sometimes. "

" I JUST SAY THINGS, and people make it out to be a much bigger deal than it really is. It's amazing, because nothing's going on. They've got a very conservative public in America, and maybe I'm just a bit too open sometimes. And if they're going to say these terrible things, you might as well do them. It's silly, but that's the age we live in. Everything is demeaning and a bit trivial, even to the extent of what they've made records sound like – they're just pieces of consumer garbage. "

" NEW FANS? . . . WHO gives a fuck about them?! To me, the whole point of making music is to satisfy myself. It's a pulsebeat, my pulsebeat, and I won't pander to anyone. "*

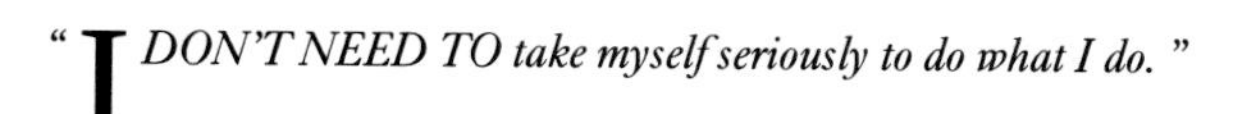

"I DON'T NEED TO take myself seriously to do what I do."

"IT'S SO EASY to be a wild man of rock when the mood takes you. I remember on the 'Whiplash Smile' tour, we were in Edmonton in Canada, and we were staying in this hotel on the tenth floor – and it was all windows! And I'd had rather a lot to drink! There were all these girls in my room, I don't remember how they got there – I suppose I asked them up. Anyway, they were getting me to drink combinations of something, wild cocktails and, I don't really know what happened, because the next thing I knew I was sitting in the room with all these huge windows smashed out. I think I'd just taken the whole place out. Which was a bit stupid really, because it was freezing, and I didn't seem to have any clothes on."

"PEOPLE PROBABLY IMAGINE I have no taste, and that I must be having sex with every Tom, Dick and Harry – or every Jill, Jane and, y'know, that I can't have no love in me or something. But the sex I sing about is *love. They don't see that and – because of AIDS and things – when people see a lifestyle like mine, they see a disease-ridden filthy place. Even though America likes rock 'n' roll, they still see it as a dangerous way of life, because they see free sex. They don't see that what we're singing about in the songs, is that we* love *people. I mean, I only have sex with people I'm having relationships with."*

"IF YOU'RE IN touch with yourself, you can use all different things and make it work for you, but the best thing is not to use anything at all. Even I *think that. I don't see any danger in trying things out, but that's not living your life on 'em! I've had trouble with drugs myself, but I don't live my life by them. I'm not taking any drugs now, and I don't need drugs to make me Billy Idol, any more than I need sex to make me Billy Idol – I just need myself and music!"*

"I TRY THINGS out, I explore 'em for a bit and then I free myself from them. I've been in danger of just having sex on the road just 'cos you've gotta do it, because there's no-one else around, but I've stopped myself – kept myself free of getting into the habit."

"IF I'D TRIED to live my life by the rock 'n' roll myth, I'd have been dead 10 years ago. I've definitely tried dangerous things but it's just like driving a car fast, you just don't do it as a habit – otherwise you're gonna crash up at the crossroads. Ha-ha . . . I've probably just missed the crossroads a couple of times, but I'm still here to talk about it."

"IT DOESN'T MATTER about money – having it, not having it. Or having clothes, or not having them. You're still left alone with yourself in the end."

"I'VE BEEN AROUND for 10 years now, and I'm never going away, not if I keep hold of what I really believe in."

"IF YOU THINK in terms of fashion, then you're always behind it. I'm just lucky that, what I personally like, hasn't been fashionable for ages. If I was like The Pet Shop Boys, I'd be behind *fashion, because that music's practically over already. The sort of drumbeats they're using, I've heard them for the last 10 years."*

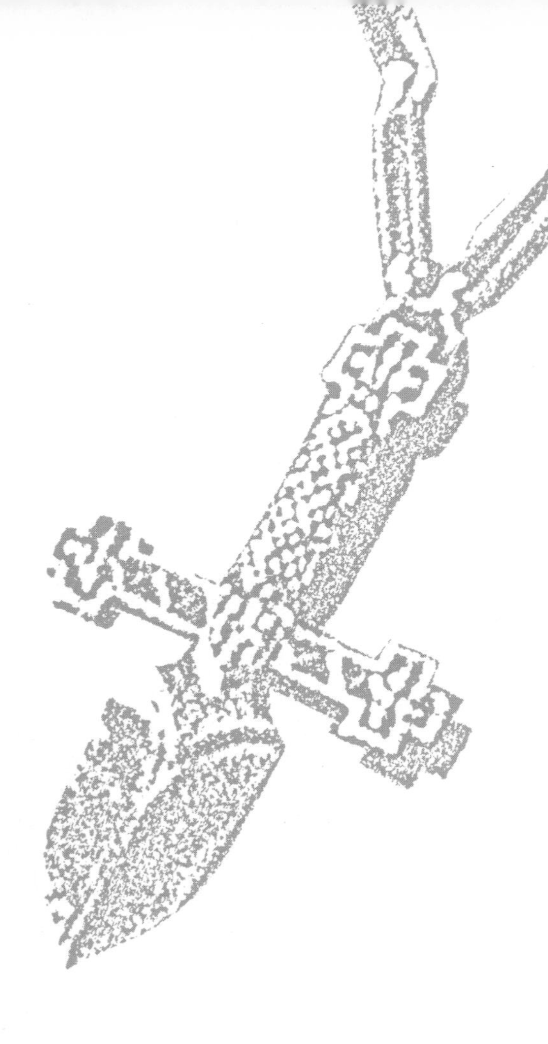

"THE THING IS, *human emotions go on – they don't just stop because, in the fifties, sixties and seventies, they sang about l[illegible] love. And even if it is re-inventing itself, there's always a new way to put it across, especially with the way technology changes. Sounds today are so incredible compared with even two years ago, that you can really produce a record that sounds fresh. Maybe it says the same as they were saying in the fifties, but it's saying it* now *in a* now *way. That's important – there's a different slant on things today.* "

"AMERICANS THINK THAT *being in the limelight keeps a rock star going – but it doesn't really. Making a great record does.* "

"OUR WORKING ARRANGEMENT *is very equal . . . with Keith Forsey, Steve and myself – we work together as a team. We're a group really. If it wasn't equal, I don't think we could make the sort of music that we do. For instance, Keith Forsey doesn't wanna make a Keith Forsey album when it comes to my music, he wants Billy Idol to make the songs. Keith wrote a song for Simple Minds called 'Don't You Forget About Me', and I said to Keith, 'Why didn't you let me sing it?' And he said, 'Well Billy, it's because I want you to write the songs, not me.' That was great, he really tries to push me, and Steve does as well. They want me to achieve something for myself . . .* "

"IN GENERATION X, *one of the things I could never do, was to improve musically. I had no-one around me to even help me understand guitar. I was living off just the knowledge I had. When I got to the States, and I met Steve, I found someone who could really help me expand musically, thus giving me a chance to focus on my singing, and to write my own lyrics. I would talk to Steve about the atmosphere I wanted in the songs – Steve could help me bring it to the surface.* "

"I'VE GOT A very basic guitar knowledge. I'm a rhythmic player, I play chords, I use the guitar to back up my voice. Steve helped me understand a lot more about keyboards, the whole musical process, even understand the technology of the studio – which was something I was always having trouble with. I'm not a technical person . . . I've got basic feelings. The same basic things that drove me on with Generation X still drive me on now. At the time, the exciting thing for me was more to be on a stage than to actually be singing!"

"NOW I FEEL like I've got a voice I can put across, whereas in those days I purely shouted and didn't even know how to sing."

"'WHIPLASH SMILE' BECAME an albatross. Even though it is *a good album, I began to realise that it wasn't leading me anywhere. It relied too much on technology, and not enough on soul."*

"I'D REALLY SORT of fried myself to a crisp in lots of ways. Even when I was in England I was a heroin addict for quite a while and, um, then interspersed with cocaine, and then a pretty heavy bout of heroin addiction around the same time as we were making 'Whiplash Smile'. I'm afraid 'Whiplash Smile' was a bit of a soulless album. Halfway through I sort of kicked heroin, and then I really went on a cocaine binge for the rest of the time. So it's er, one of the most soulless pieces of shit I think anybody could make. The only thing that saved it was, I think, 'To Be A Lover' and 'Sweet Sixteen', maybe."

"ALL IN ALL, it's time for a change, time for a new me . . ."

1987

february

Old Gold Records re-issue a couple of classic Generation X numbers, and 'King Rocker' along with 'Valley Of The Dolls' finally achieve commercial recognition.
Meanwhile Billy's latest single, 'Don't Need A Gun', is released by Chrysalis in a variety of formats – all of which add up to further Top 30 success.
A string of live shows are lined-up.

may

The tuneful 'Sweet Sixteen' is released. Although a playlist mega-hit, the song remarkably stops at 17 in the home chart.
When Billy discloses that 'Sweet Sixteen' has been inspired by 16-year-old Tammi Gordon – to whom the singer has taken something of a liking – Perri Lister (they're together again at this stage) throws a bit of a tantrum.

june

McDonald Bros Records release an album of early Generation X sessions, entitled 'Original Generation X'.

august

Billy hits the road again, but declines to play in the UK.

september

Autumn brings another Idol re-release, and another smash hit. His first ever solo single, 'Mony Mony', this time backed with a live version of another cover, 'Shakin' All Over', cruises to number seven in the UK.

october

Stateside gossip suggests Sir William could be about to become a dad . . . It's also whispered, once again, that he may have developed a drug 'problem'.

november

Billy's live version of 'Mony Mony' replaces Tiffany's 'I Think We're Alone Now' at the top of the US chart. (Amazingly both songs had originally been hits in the sixties for Tommy James And The Shondells.) Billy celebrates by buying a new Harley Davidson. Oops.
Billy decides to make his permanent home in Los Angeles, where he quickly gets into the local trends – like buying running shoes, giving up 'drugs' and going to the gym a lot. He also christens his Harley 'Rude Dude', and starts cruising L.A. with Keith Forsey.
Rumours suggest that Billy is in the process of changing management companies – intending to sign a long-term deal with Tony Dimitriades of Look-Out Management. Tony, a well-respected figure in US rock, is already responsible for the affairs of Yes, Tom Petty and Stevie Nicks. His partner, Elliot Roberts, is the man-that-matters for Bob Dylan and Neil Young, among others . . .

december

Billy and Perri spend Christmas scuba-diving in Jamaica where, at one stage, they're attacked by a vicious barracuda. Billy saves the day when he shoots the offending fish with a speargun . . . It must be true, it's in the papers.

"I'VE HAD A lot of girls in my life, and I'm sure I've got a couple of kids out there somewhere. So far none of them has told me I'm the daddy of her child, but I'm always scared when I go on tour that it's going to happen."

"ONE OF THE reasons I moved from New York to Los Angeles, was because it seemed there was a bit more of a scene going on, where you could meet musicians. And my producer, Keith Forsey, lived out here – and he knew a lot of musicians as well."

"I'D GOT TO the end of my musical life in New York. I knew Steve Stevens was gonna go off and do his solo stuff. I knew right from the beginning of 'Whiplash Smile' that eventually he was gonna go off and do his own band. So I knew I was going to have to find new people to play with, and I felt I'd already played with the best people in Manhattan. In L.A. there were still people who believed that rock 'n' roll was still great."

"I LIKED WHAT was going on in the metal scene in L.A. – with Motley Crue, Guns N' Roses, and everybody like that. At least Guns N' Roses have the balls to be who they want. They're not sitting around worrying, 'Oh, are we gonna sell fewer records because we talk about heroin and all?' "

"I HUNG OUT with Axl one night. At the time, Guns N' Roses were going through this whole thing about whether or not they were gonna stay together. I felt like an old man saying, 'No, keep your band together baby. Don't blow it now man . . .' "

"I DON'T WANT anything to do with heavy metal . . . it's just dinosaur ignoramus music."

"BY THE TIME I got to L.A., I had this horrendous pain underneath my shoulder blades. My energy level had dropped off quite a bit, as a result of 10 years of boozing and roving and sleeping in the back of vans and fuck knows where. Every time I tried to play my guitar I had these terrible pains because my body was so weak. So I had to ask the question, 'Do I want to slide into middle age gracefully and give it all up, or do I want to keep on rocking?' I finally realised I had to do something to put some energy back into my body. I hated the idea of working-out, but I can't be the person I want to be unless I do work-out. And if I didn't do it, I wouldn't be here."

"I'M JUST NOT hung-up on (drugs) any more. That's why I came out here (to California) in the first place, to take control of my life and to fight against all the things that can trap you – and take your natural spirit away. If you're drowning yourself in something, you're drowning everything, and that means you're not really facing up to life. So that's what I'm doing. It's not a question of doing it because I have to, it's more like I just wanted it that way. I was getting very bogged down in what I was doing, and resorting to 'things'."

"I ALWAYS WORE *the leather, I just never could afford the bike! I was a bloke in leather* looking *for a bike – a rebel without a horse!*"

"WE WENT ON this charity ride – for muscular dystrophy – it was such a beautiful sight . . . Imagine 2,000 Harleys, five miles ahead of you, going 80 miles-an-hour through the Hollywood hills . . . It's like a new club for me."

"GETTING A MOTORBIKE was a great way of changing my lifestyle. I had to depend on myself to get around. And it's a great way of giving yourself a thrill, instead of drugs or alcohol. In California, it's an essential way of getting to places really *fast."*

"I DECIDED I'D had it with the constant round of cleaning up and getting ill again. It had affected my mind to the extent where I wasn't the same person. A lot of people went through that who came out of punk rock. Sid Vicious wasn't the only one, and I think heroin was one of the things that probably killed punk rock . . . So when I got out to Los Angeles, part of the idea was to hang onto the side of me that I loved the most, which was the energetic, happy side, whose first love was music and being alive."

"I THOUGHT THAT buying my Harley Davidson was a great way to commemorate having a number one single. I never had a bike in England – I never had the money. I had the clothes, *but I could never afford the bike. I'm glad I started working-out because a Harley Davidson is, like, 700 pounds, and if you drop your bike and can't pick it up, you know you're a bit of an asshole."*

1988

january

Yet another new/old single finds its way into the Top 20. This time it's 'Hot In The City', revamped as a trailer for the forthcoming 'Best Of' album.
The single's accompanying video falls foul of the censors however, especially in America, where there's a 'bit of a reaction' to seeing a scantily dressed pregnant woman (Perri), being bound up against a gigantic crucifix. In light of recent pressure from the Washington Wives, as well as from other fast-rising action groups, MTV insists on *nine* specific cuts to the promo. Billy responds in typical fashion, so the video isn't shown at all.
Ho-hum . . . What's *really* shocking to most of his fans however, is the news that Billy has accepted an offer from Joni Mitchell to record a duet ('Dancing Clown') on her latest album. Blimey.

february

A second interview with Billy is released on record. Catalogued as 'Interview Picture Disc', it's produced by a company called Music And Media.

march

The much-mooted video, 'More Vital Idol', hits the window displays – crucifixes an' all.

april

By now, Billy is spending much of his spare time working on new material, for an album scheduled for next year.

june

Perri Lister gives birth to Billy's son, whom they name Willem Wolfe. The nipper weighs in at an extremely healthy 8lbs 6ozs.
After much speculation, 'Idol Songs: 11 Of The Best' finds its way into the shops. Running order is: 'Rebel Yell'/'Hot In The City'/'White Wedding'/'Eyes Without A Face'/'Catch My Fall'/'Mony Mony'/'To Be A Lover'/'Sweet Sixteen'/'Flesh For Fantasy'/'Don't Need A Gun'/'Dancing With Myself'. The CD features additional extended mixes of 'Eyes Without A Face', 'To Be A Lover', 'Don't Need A Gun' and 'Mony Mony'.
Another posthumous Generation X album emerges. This time it's 'Generation X Live', once again promoted by McDonald Bros.

july

Billy spends time rehearsing, and re-working songs under construction.
The schedule's not too hectic however, and the rocker still finds time to join Harley Davidson designer, Willie G. Davidson, on the first leg of a charity ride from L.A. to Milwaukee. The event marks the bike company's 85th anniversary.
Mixing business with pleasure now, Billy draws a temporary halt to studio work, by instigating another little road trip – this time for the benefit of his brand new band. Riding to Hanford, California – Billy, Mark Younger-Smith (guitar), Phil Soussan (bass) and Keith Forsey (filling in on drums), play a set of five numbers at a local club. One of them is a cover of The Doors classic, 'L.A. Woman'.

august

'Catch My Fall' is the latest single, and in failing to reach the Top 50, it becomes Billy's first true flop for yonks.
Another 'Interview Picture Disc' does the rounds. This time Baktabak is responsible.
Billy reportedly turns down a $1 million sponsorship deal with Sony.

september

Billy goes into the recording studio with guitarist Mark Younger-Smith (from Charlie Sexton's band), bassist Phil Soussan (the former Ozzy Osbourne sidekick), and drummer Mike Baird (ex-Journey, *snigger*). Still with producer Keith Forsey, much is made of the fact that Billy is no longer working with guitarist, and long-term sidekick, Steve Stevens. But Steve is now working on his *own* material, as well as playing occasional session guitar for Michael Jackson!

november

Billy joins Julian Lennon and Charlie Sexton at a benefit show in L.A. It's an all-out effort to trace the 'hit and run' driver responsible for the death of a motorcycling friend, Lee Selwyn – the 26-year-old Californian disc jockey. It's hoped that the thousands of dollars raised may be used as a reward for anyone providing useful information. Back in the studio, Billy is said to be making real headway on the new songs. After recording "finished versions" of 'Love Child', 'Trouble With The Sweet Stuff', 'Prodigal Son Blues', 'Love Unchained' and 'Licence To Thrill', there is great optimism for the new album to be "out by May", ho-ho-ho . . .

december

Idol appears to take a break from recording, and "out by May" looks like a fib to rival "your cheque's in the post."

Along with Rod Stewart, Cyndi Lauper, Aerosmith, Suzanne Vega, Bobby McFerrin and INXS, Billy attends MTV's annual music awards bash in Los Angeles. Also present is Elvira, America's late-night horror movie presenter, who's forced to spend the best part of the evening removing Billy's face from her bosom.

The same month sees Billy team up with the likes of Bob Dylan, Tom Petty, Tracy Chapman and Jerry Garcia, when he performs at an all-acoustic charity concert in San Francisco. In aid of the Bridge School for handicapped children, the event is inspired by Neil Young's wife, who has two children with cerebral palsy. Accompanied by Mark Younger-Smith on guitar, and Keith Forsey on single snare drum, His Idolness plays 'Sweet Sixteen', 'To Be A Lover', 'Prodigal Son Blues' and the old Generation X song, 'Untouchables'.

" *MTV AND I have had an excellent relationship. But now they've taken my 'Hot In The City' video the wrong way, and want to change my vision . . . It represents the longing, lust, fantasies and resentment that obsess the lonely.* "

" *I WAS DETERMINED to shoot the video here, in New York, because . . . it's like saying I've made this my musical home for seven years. My musical home has* always *been here. 'Hot In The City' was always a homage to coming from England and being accepted here immediately.* "

" *I'VE ALWAYS PREFERRED to script my own videos . . . Since the song's mine anyway, I like to think I'm clever enough to concoct some sort of visual* – and *make sense with it.* "

" *IT'S FUNNY REALLY that now I'm the bad boy of rock – back in England I was the 'clean punk'!!*

"MONEY? NO, *I don't think about it. Never wanted all that flash stuff – it's a bit of a bother really. I don't need that much.* "

"I LAUGHED, AND *I was shocked, when Joni Mitchell invited me to record with her. I wasn't sure that it was the right thing to do, but then she read me the lyrics. It was close to what I would sing about . . . so why not?* "

"IT WAS ONLY *with the birth of my son that I had a reversal and found a reason to love.* "

"I GAVE OVER *quite a lot of time, a year or so, to being with Perri . . . It was a natural home birth, and having him certainly threw a new set of emotions into the everyday ballpark . . . I suppose it makes you a little more philosophical. I wanted to write about the excitement of being a life-giver, of creating life.* "

"SHE DIDN'T TAKE *any drugs or* anything, *so it really was a natural birth. At one point, after seven hours, I started crying because it was watching someone you love – really in pain. And then I thought, 'What are* you *crying for? You've got to help her mate!' I cut the umbilical cord and everything, and I just saw this beautiful, magical side of life – the* birth *of a life. It was so wonderful it was almost like* I *was born again.* "

"WHEN OLD WILLY *was born, I started to think differently about various aspects of my life. 'Course, I can still be wild and crazy – I'll always be a bit of a nutcase – but I've got my son to think about now . . . Instead of wasting it all away, I'm now thinking much more about how I spend my time.* "

"FANCY ME BEING a dad! My kids'll have to wear suits to rebel against me!"

"STEVE STEVENS IS a very accomplished musician, and anybody who's got the talent will, in the end, want to explore things for themselves. And it's just as well in a way, because a musician shouldn't be limited to playing somebody else's vision. He was bound to wonder what Steve Stevens' stuff would sound like."

"I JUST DIDN'T connect with Steve Stevens on 'Whiplash Smile' like I did on 'Rebel Yell'. I don't know why. Six or seven years of playing with someone is quite a long time and we just lost a bit of the magic. Meeting Mark Younger-Smith gave me a lynchpin, someone I could work with by forming a sound and an idea for this album . . . Mark likes rhythm 'n' blues, which is a different kind of guitar sound for me, but when it clicks, it's great!"

"CERTAIN TYPES OF guitar playing don't always fit in with what I'm trying to do. And with Steve really wanting to go off and do his own records, it stopped the whole thing from working – which is a shame, but that's what happens with musicians. That's the exciting part about it. When it clicks, it's great, but when it doesn't you're better off getting on with someone else. My move to Los Angeles meant we were physically in different towns, and that's what really finished it."

"I'M HOOKED (ON Wella Hard Rock Hairspray). I have crate-loads sent over to New York. I must use at least a pint a day on my hair."

"APPARENTLY EVERYBODY'S OUT there waiting for my next album – big fucking deal! The wait isn't gonna kill anybody, and it's certainly gonna hurt me more if I put out shit. 'Cos then I'd be standing there going, 'Well, why am I doing this?' So I'd rather wait four years, or three years, or two months – and then finish it. Or if it's right, do it tomorrow."

"PRODUCTION WISE, THE next album is going to be a lot rawer than 'Whiplash Smile'. It's first and foremost a rock 'n' roll album, but there's a bit of the blues in there . . . And that should frighten everyone a bit!"

"IT'S REALLY HILARIOUS for someone like me to be at something like that (the Bridge School charity show), isn't it? It was so funny to go up there in front of a load of old hippies. It was a real laugh drawing up at the concert and, instead of there being a load of raging punks, it was like the most tie-dyed thing I'd ever seen. So I went on and said, 'I know I've got my leather trousers on, but underneath I've got a pair of tie-dyed underpants . . . I don't think they liked my language."

1989

january

Billy returns to work on the album.

march

In London, staff at *Q* magazine hear reports of 'something decidedly fishy' going on between Billy and his record company. The suggestion is that, contrary to the official line, the idle rocker *has* finished his new album, has titled it 'Charmed Life', but is refusing to hand over the work to his representatives at the label. With speculation mounting as to the financial security of the company, it seems Billy could be concerned for the promotional budget of his latest *Meisterwerk*.

june

Billy is forced to pay out nearly £15,000 compensation to a woman who was trampled during his 1987 show at the Memorial Coliseum, Portland in Oregon. Lucy Hammond had reportedly received multiple injuries when the audience stormed the stage – supposedly at the singer's invitation.

august

The world sees what Billy's former sidekick is capable of, when 'Steve Stevens Atomic Playboys' is released.

Billy joins a celebrity cast for a special performance of The Who's rock opera *Tommy*, staged at L.A.'s Universal Amphitheater. Playing the part of Tommy's obnoxious and sadistic Cousin Kevin, the peroxide star lines up alongside Elton John (the Pinball Wizard), Steve Winwood (the Hawker), Patti LaBelle (the Acid Queen), Phil Collins (Uncle Ernie) and, of course, The Who. $2 million are raised for children's charities – and for the rock 'n' roll 'Hall Of Fame'.

september

Along with former punk guru and Sex Pistols' manager, Malcolm McLaren, Billy is invited to contribute material to the musical score of a new movie – starring the latest US cult heroes . . . The Teenage Mutant Ninja Turtles! The former comic strip stars are already big news in the States and, despite everyone's best efforts, are destined for world domination by the end of the decade.

october

Rolling Stone magazine announces the end of Billy's on-off relationship with long-time girlfriend Perri Lister – actress, singer, dancer, choreographer and *mother* of Billy's son Willem Wolfe. Meanwhile Billy, who is already being linked with another actress – Maria Conchita Alonso – goes on holiday to Thailand, allegedly wrecks a hotel room and is promptly charged with criminal damage.

Returning to Britain by the end of the month though, Billy's soon back in favour when he appears at the London leg of The Who's *Tommy* Appeal. Still talking 'bout degeneration, Billy is again part of a cast of thousands, in an extravagant show presented at the prestigious Royal Albert Hall.

november

Billy is attacked by a knife-wielding 'fan' outside London's notorious Wag Club. Wounds to his leg are bad enough to require treatment at Westminster Hospital.

december

Back in the studio, Billy is *still* working on his new album. Rumours abound that the record has already cost $1.5 million to make, and that the record company don't like it. The rumours are strenuously denied.

The year closes with word of a possible role for Billy in Oliver Stone's movie about The Doors. The serious hacks say it's just a rumour, so everyone else knows it must be true.

"*ONE OF THE things that I really wanted to do with this next album, was to make sure that I had live musicians on it. When we recorded 'Whiplash Smile', we used all the technological tricks we could. The album was more or less just made with me, Keith Forsey and Steve Stevens. And of course, the thing about using all the machines – although they have your personality because* you're *playing them – you're not getting the 'bounce-off' of other personalities, you're sort of bouncing-off yourself. It's like jerking-off. I mean, I'd much rather somebody else was jerking me off, than me doing it.* "

"*THE NEW ALBUM isn't taking* that *long y'know . . . After all, I've still got two years on Tears For Fears.* "

"*I LIKE THE idea that the next Billy Idol record is going to come out in 1990. I'll be able to put in my advertising, 'Three Decades Of Billy Idol!'* "

"I'VE JUST DONE this song called 'Trouble With The Sweet Stuff'. It's my song for every AA, CA, SA person in the world. It's for everybody who's forced to give up the thing that they love – whether it's love or drugs or booze. Of course, the biggest one is love. It seems like everybody's got trouble with the sweet stuff at the moment."

"GENERATION X HAD a song called 'Your Generation' in 1977, when The Who seemed to have seen their best days – but really we were fans, and were a little bit hurt. We started to get to know Keith Moon and Pete Townshend. One day I met Keith at a charity event, and talked him into coming down to a rehearsal with me. We did 'I Can See For Miles', 'Anyhow, Anywhere', 'My Generation', and then 'Your Generation' and a couple more of ours – he didn't know them, and he was all over the place, but it was great. Later in New York I bumped into Pete, and he was really supportive of what I was doing at a time when I really needed it. So, when they were working out who should play Cousin Kevin . . . It was my way of saying 'Thanks a lot.' I was the biggest fan up there, and I know a lot of people wondered what the fuck I thought I was doing, but basically I'd played with Keith Moon years ago, and there I was playing with the rest of the band. I was proud to be there with people who'd written and performed some of rock's greatest songs."

"I NEVER WANTED to be home with the pipe and the slippers and the armchair. I want my life to have the feeling that everything's up in the air sometimes. I was with my last girlfriend for nine years (!), and the great thing that cemented my relationship with her was having my son, little Willy Wolfe. We know we love each other, whether we're together or not, with the music we're always going to be apart at some point, thank God. But I love the idea that we cemented something we thought was beautiful. My son is like a great postscript."

"I NEVER WANT to get married – not if I can help it. I think it's boring, everybody saying, 'Oh, you've settled down now'."

"PERRI IS AN actress, a dancer and a singer. She's very much rooted in the theatrical world, while I'm rooted in this musical world. It's like we were dragged apart by those two things. The best part is that we both love our son, so he's getting love all the time. We're not fighting over him, or about him, so it's been alright. We're still really good friends in many ways, and that's the testament of Willem Wolfe to our relationship. He is something great that came out of it, even as the relationship itself was being cast asunder."

"I WAS TRYING to live almost a married kind of existence, with a son and a house. And when we split up, it threw my whole world a curve. When something that massive happens in my life, suddenly I have to take stock of everything again. I have to reinterpret how I see my life. And that made writing songs quite different. It took me a while to come up with a song like 'Loveless'. It takes time to put those emotional upsets into perspective, so that I can write songs about them. My songs are always *reflective of something that's happened in the past."*

"I DON'T KNOW, I sort of need to experience life to write songs. I'm not one of those people who can sit down every day for three hours to write a song. So there can be a bit of time in between – until I feel I've got something special. I can write a million songs a year – it's just trying to write a good *one. That's the point. It takes a while for me to find something special enough, an idea I can take and make into something that's really me. If something dramatic happens to change my life though, that makes a difference."*

"YOU HAVE TO follow your own pursuits, one way or another. One day you wake up and you love the fact that you're all alone, and the next day you wake up and you wish that you were with somebody. You're always searching for the things you haven't got. I think that's where the drive comes in though . . . "

" 'CHARMED LIFE' IS 45 minutes of indecent exposure. It follows the tone of the last song I wrote for the album, '311 Man'. 311 is the police code for flashing one's private parts. What better description of rock 'n' roll. "

1990

january

Rumours abound that Billy Idol's next album – his first collection of new titles for three-and-a-half years – is to be released in the Spring.
Billy wins substantial damages against the *News Of The World*, following libellous allegations concerning his behaviour at a charity event in aid of muscular dystrophy. Reports in the newspaper that Billy had behaved 'outrageously and indecently in front of handicapped children' seemed to be at odds with everyone else's version of the event – including that of the charity organisers!

february

Billy is in celebratory mood, as the continually delayed 'Charmed Life' album is at last completed. He and producer Keith Forsey finally call it a wrap on the night of the fifth, little knowing what the next day would bring.
The singer tackles the following morning much like any other. Starting with a customary work-out, he leaps aboard his trusted Harley and cruises down the drive of his Hollywood Hills home. First port of call is to be Conway Studios, where he's agreed to pick up the final mixes of 'Charmed Life'. As we now know, of course, Billy doesn't make it. Driving south to Melrose Avenue he finds the crossing at Fountain Avenue busier than expected. Before he can assess the situation further, a fellow traveller meets him broadside and sends the victim plummeting to the ground. As is his wont, Billy isn't wearing a crash helmet. He looks death in the face – and survives.
The remainder of the month sees Billy in hospital, undertaking a series of operations aimed at repairing a broken left arm and, more seriously, a compound fracture of the right leg. With the aid of the most modern techniques in reconstructive surgery and skin grafting, the limb is thankfully saved.
While recuperating at Cedars-Sinai Medical Center, Idol discovers he's across the hall from cancer patient Sammy Davis Jr . . .
Billy receives hospital visits from Jack Nicholson and Jon Bon Jovi. The latter says he understands just how Billy feels, 'cos he was 'once in hospital to have his tonsils removed' . . . Oh, and Cyndi Lauper sends some get well balloons.
After five operations, Idol finally hobbles out of hospital on state-of-the-art crutches – lucky to be alive and, miraculously, still kicking.

april

Armed with a walking stick, Billy accepts the offer from Oliver Stone (director of *Platoon*, *Wall Street* and *Born On The Fourth Of July*) to play a small part in the film-maker's adventurous Doors movie. Forced to decline an earlier offer of a more demanding role (because of his accident), Billy now accepts the minor part of a composite character, derived from several of Morrison's known acquaintances.
Billy's 'Charmed Life' album is finally released, to encouraging reviews. Running order is: 'The Loveless'/'Pumping On Steel'/'Prodigal Blues'/'L.A. Woman'/'Trouble With The Sweet Stuff'/'Cradle Of Love'/'Mark Of Caine'/'Endless Sleep'/'Love Unchained'/'The Right Way'/'License To Thrill'.
Critics can't help but herald the lyrical content of the album, especially in the light of recent

events. Understandably much is made of the track, 'Love Unchained', which had been written for a pal who'd died, *a-hem*, in a bike crash – while in 'Pumping On Steel', the lines 'I've got to ride/I might die tonight' also merit obvious attention. As for the old Marty Wilde tear-jerker, 'Endless Sleep' . . . it might have been the most prophetic swansong in rock 'n' roll's all too accident-prone history. But happily, it isn't.

With tabloids telling tales of Billy's new-found 'respect for life', 'love of God', and 'all-round maturity', the star orders a brand new chopper to be custom-made – according to one report – in an attractive shade of blood red! Hmmm. Overseeing the design seems to alleviate much of the boredom his injuries have provided.

Although widely believed to have calmed down, and 'matured' as a human being, Billy embarks on a whole string of TV and newspaper interviews intent on proving the opposite.

With 'Charmed Life' climbing to 15 in the album charts, the single – 'Cradle Of Love' – fails to make the Top 30, even though the *video* for the song is delivered to reviewers by stripper-gram girls!

july

Billy is featured alongside the likes of George Harrison, Paul Simon and Guns N' Roses, on an album released to raise money for the Romanian Angel Appeal. Entitled 'Nobody's Child' all proceeds go to help the country's ever growing number of orphaned children.

Limping back into the limelight then, rock's least reluctant hero rehearses a new live band in preparation for a major tour. The line-up consists of Mark Younger-Smith (guitar), Tal Bergman (drums), Larry Seymour (bass) and Bonnie Hayes (keyboards).

august

Billy's version of The Doors' classic, 'L.A. Woman' is released as a single.

Meanwhile, as the singer's world jaunt kicks off in North America, plans are being finalised for the European schedule later in the year.

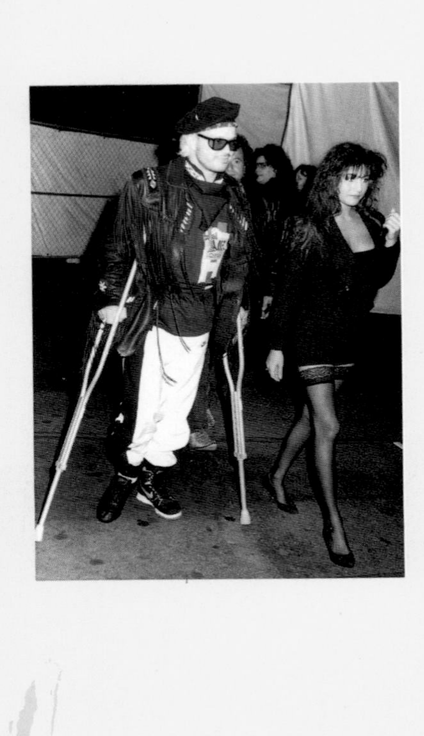

november

Part of that European schedule (a couple of dates in Sweden and Denmark) is cancelled, as Billy falls foul of an eye problem. Diagnosed as 'lacerated corneas', the malaise is reputedly the result of wearing dodgy contact lenses.

With dates already lined-up in the UK for next month, fans are anxiously preparing for Billy's first *ever* home-based tour as a solo artist! Everyone just hopes his leg will hold out – and that when he finally gets to Blighty, he'll remember to drive on the left!

"*THE GREAT THING about the Harley, is that you're not really riding it for speed. You can cruise* or *go fast. But if you only want to go fast, you should get one of those Suzuki things. We call them 'organ-donors'. But with a Harley, you're really watching out for yourself . . .* "

"*AS SOON AS I entered the intersection, I went – 'Fuck! It's a main road!' Then I see this car coming, and the next thing I know I'm lying at the side of the gutter. I was conscious almost the whole time. I lifted up my hand and it was all withered and hanging, then I picked my leg up and it looked like a fucking stump. And just as I did that, someone came over and told me not to move, and I went 'Lie still? Aaarrgghhh!'* "

"*I REALLY DIDN'T have time to think about whether or not I was going to die. It was all pretty quick . . . The first thing I thought was, 'I can think'.* "

"*IT WASN'T REALLY anybody's fault. There was minimal damage to the woman who was driving the car that I crashed into. I was the one who copped it.* "

"*IT WAS PRETTY wild. The leg bone had gone straight through the jeans –* whoooooaar*! – and ripped the muscle to shreds. Wild! Ha-ha! And there was blood all over everything, and I kept blacking out, and I was in all this pain, and I came to on the operating table with somebody with a pair of scissors going up my shirt, cutting the clothes off me. And all I could think about was – thank the* fuck *I didn't wear one of my favourite leather jackets.* "

"*I WASN'T WEARING a crash helmet. I heard this massive bang when I got hit, and everybody says if you hear the bang, you're alright.* "

"*I HAVE THIS great big hole in my leg – you can look right in and see the bone and everything. That's the thing that was really dodgy about it all, the fact that there was such a big hole in my leg – and they really didn't know if they could cover it up. I even asked the physiotherapist if he had ever seen anybody with a bigger hole in their leg.* "

"*I'VE ALWAYS HAD a real positive outlook on things, so I never really thought, 'You could lose your leg,' or 'You'll never walk again,' although in reality it could be some time before I can walk properly.* "

"*I WAS LYING there in hospital with pins through my leg, sticking out like Frankenstein bolts, and a great big hole the size of a cricket ball – kind of pussy shaped actually – and you could see the bone. I was doped up on morphine. It didn't really occur to me what might happen.* "

"*THEY HAD TO put a steel rod in my leg. They shaved back the bone and, to fit it in, they took some chips of bone off my hip and put it around the steel rod.* "

"*TEN YEARS AGO they might not have been able to do what they've done for me, but my friends were more aware of the situation than I was. They put you on this morphine PCM machine, a drip-feed you can administer yourself every time it hurts. I was ding-donged! I was ready to buy one and take it on the road with me.* "

"*MY CAREER WASN'T supposed to last this long anyway. Of all the original punk rockers, I was always the least credible. So 'Charmed Life' has* that *joke in it.* "

"*THE ACCIDENT MADE me think. I really do think that life itself is kind of magical and mysterious. It's like Oscar Wilde said – it's not the* invisible *that's got the mystical side to it, it's the* visible. *And the album is about how great life is, and how bad it is just to throw it away, which I almost did.* "

"MAYBE 'CHARMED LIFE' is a parting shot. I mean, everybody could have been hearing this record after I was dead. It's like I've seen that side of it, and it's great to be alive – which is what the album was saying in the first place."

"THANK GOD I finished the album. Everyone would have thought Keith Forsey did it all again!"

"THE WILD THING is that now *I can really appreciate it all. I can see other people who have had accidents, and they can't walk again – what a terrible blow it must be. This is nothing like not being able to walk forever, but at the same time I got a real definite taste. I went through the whole glad-to-be-alive bit just after the accident, because it's all so pertinent right there and then. You know, 'You've almost bit the bullet' kind of thing. When I woke up alongside the curb, it really made me think, 'Wow, I'm still here.' And so I really went through a real joy, glad to be alive period."*

"I HEARD SAMMY (Davis Jr) was feeling a lot better and was ready to check-out, so I sent him a photo and signed it, 'Glad to hear you're out of here . . .'"

"WHILE I WAS in hospital, I got letters from people aged between three and 73, all saying where they'd heard my music for the first time. And it really did make me think that, y'know, I do have a gift – even if it's only for a few people."

"I'VE GOTTEN A lot of great letters, and all the goodwill really cheers you up. Because one way or another, especially with all the drugs and morphine, you kind of go through a bit of an up and down state of mind. Especially right after the operation. Just the fact that I know there were a lot of people wishing me well, has really made me feel great."

"IT'S FUNNY, 'COS a lot of people think I did 'Charmed Life' after *the motorcycle accident, but it's the other way around – and it made me feel really happy when I woke up from the anaesthetic, and I was still on the old morphine, and I played the album. I almost got quite choked up that I really was singing about the sort of things that, if you did have a fucking nasty near death accident and you're lying in hospital really in agony and it's just 'orrible, and now you're cold turkeying and you've gotta shit where you sleep and you're just pouring with sweat and it's 'orrible – then there on the record, it's saying, 'No, don't give in! Don't ever give up the power to love' and all that shit. It made me go 'Cor, I* can *like my own records! There* is *something good about them!"*

"I'M ESPECIALLY PROUD of the track 'Prodigal Blues' . . . It's my father talking to me, and me talking to Willem. By being angry, mad and crazy at times, I've shouted for an answer and all I've got back was my own echo. What I'm saying to Willem is what my father said to me – everybody has to leave the security of things they love, to find out what they're all about. But you don't necessarily have to destroy yourself to do it."

"IN THE PAST, I've been a little unwilling to show all my personality. I wanted to sing mostly about hurt rather than love. I'm not like that any more, and my music is changing as I am."

" A LOT OF the songs I've sung have had elements of frustration and anger. It's great to finally be able to approach the other sides of what I really feel . . . 'Prodigal Blues' is a love song between parent and child. I think it shows people that I can sing about other things with the same sort of passion and drive, the same sort of rock 'n' roll spirit, without it having to be something I'm angry about. "

" TEN YEARS AGO, I didn't even know if I'd be alive today. Seriously, I don't think my songs of that time were as anti-emotion as people thought . . . Like, the 'Generation X' album had 'Untouchables', which was about losing your friends, the emotional ties you had with them. You can only shout and spit at people for so long. You look into the eyes of a young person and see the love flowing, and you realise that life's more complicated than that. "

" I COULD IMAGINE myself thinking, 'Blimey what's happened to Billy Idol?' But I'm still able to put these feelings into a rock 'n' roll context, where it's a little more swashbuckling, rather than just talking about it like this is the cold light of day. I'm leaning a little bit more to the emotional side, and without doing this, I couldn't go back to screaming about things. "

" THE WAY I'VE been living the last couple of years, has meant that I've looked back at my life and reflected on it a lot more – to sing about what's actually happening to me right now at this moment – and it's led to these kind of thoughts. But I'm not saying every album's gonna be like this! "

" MY NEXT TOUR is going to have no redeeming features whatsoever. "

" ALL THE GOOD things in life, including my relationship and my music, were at rock bottom. And I just had to sort it all out. One great thing is that I think I've got a musical gift that makes people excited, and helps them when they're happy or when they're sad. And it's nothing to be sneered at – at least not by me. I don't mind if other people laugh – great! . . . I've got my purpose in life back again. "

" WHAT THIS ACCIDENT has done for me, is made me happy to be alive. And I'm even happier that I've got a really great way to show people that – with my music. And I'm able to enjoy doing it. "

" WHEN YOU LOSE the use of one of your body parts, other parts become stronger. My sex life has been great since the accident! "

" I'M HAVING THIS high-tail chopper custom-made for me right now . . . I just hope I don't hear that crash every time I get on. "

"*THE THING I'M worried about, is that I was planning on* Easy Rider*-ing across the States on my US tour. We're gonna take the bikes on a trailer behind the bus, get out in the middle of nowhere, and ride alongside. Y'know, sort of Malcolm Forbes-it across country. That'll be the next time I get on a bike, and you can be sure it won't be in the same sort of built-up urban area.*"

"*I'LL BE BACK on a bike soon. I still like all the danger and unexpectedness that comes with riding a motorcycle, just like in rock 'n' roll. See, I don't think that you have to grow up – I think you have to grow* into *yourself. If I grew up I'd stop being me, and I wouldn't be any good to anybody.*"

"*IT'S NOTHING to do with trying to be this, or doing that, or something or other. It's actually expedient and, with a few mates, it makes it even more fun. The other thing is, imagine, this is the country of shorts and polyester – because it's so bloody hot. So how else are you gonna go about in leather if you're not on a motorcycle?!* I *don't wanna walk around in fucking shorts!*"

"*I'VE BEEN GOING to bed really early, pushing the time along. I've already had it with this fucking sitting around watching films. I've gone through my Elvis season, my James Bond season . . . I've seen 'em all. I could be out there rockin' instead of being fucked up, which is a shame really.*"

"I *WAS WATCHING this* Elvis '68 *thing on cable or something, and I could see Elvis was kinda walking through things like 'All Shook Up'... but at the end he sings this song, 'If I Could Dream'. He takes this song, and he belts it out so fucking great, and when you get to the middle bit I was going wild! And it's funny, right at the end of it he stands back and, instead of being all bravado and 'Ha-ha-ha showed you', he stands back like the little schoolboy who sang 'Old Shep' in 1952 at Tupelo, Mississippi – as if a school-teacher was going to come on and say, 'Thank you very much Elvis, you sung that very well, 10 out of 10...' And even lying there with me ol' broken leg and everything, it made me think, 'Oh fucking yes', it's like when I went to see The Sex Pistols and all that. Yes! That's what we want...* Passion*!*"

"T*HAT'S THE TROUBLE with life, it leads you on. You need that passion to want to stay alive, but your desires are going to lead you into some kind of destruction.*"

"T*HE WORST THING about the accident was that I nearly lost the movie with Oliver Stone. I couldn't believe it when he gave me the part, because I realised I* loved *this guy's films. I don't care what I do – I'll be in the background sweeping up.*"

"I *WAS SUPPOSED to play Tom Baker, this kind of evil friend of Jim Morrison's, who eggs him on to do all these bad things. Now, I'm sort of a composite character, who isn't a real person. It's a lesser role at the moment, but I'm not really in a position where I could play a larger part. But this is my chance to play a rock 'n' roll character who's neither a singer nor a rock star – and it's perfect for me.*"

"J*IM MORRISON MADE a couple of films, and he had a little crew of friends who helped him make them. I'm playing a character sort of* representative *of those people. My character is a bit of a biker, so it's quite likely that he could have screwed his leg up.*"

"I*N THE MOVIE I've got long hair and sideburns and totally hippie clothing. I look the way I did when I was 13 or 14. No-one will recognise me!... In fact, I'm thinking of keeping it up for a while. Y'know, like going out to places where nobody would know it's Billy Idol. I wear this Navaho Indian shirt and all – it's a real period piece!*"

"I *THINK DANNY Sugerman, who wrote the book that the movie's based on, felt there should be a few* real *rock 'n' roll people in the film, to give it the spice of reality. What's great to me, is that someone like Oliver Stone has that belief in my ability, whatever it is. It's a great chance. It's great to be in a rock 'n' roll film as well. I love rock 'n' roll films. And I've got a feeling that this is gonna be one of the best rock 'n' roll films ever made.*"

"*OLIVER'S DONE SOME great things with the script, using Jim Morrison's music and poetry in conjunction with his life, in order to explain why he wrote the songs he did. There's every damn Doors song in the film, and they're not in chronological order. It starts with 'Riders On The Storm', and it ends with 'When The Music's Over'. 'Hello I Love You' is in a scene in 1965 when he's hanging out in Venice, not in 1968 when he wrote it. It's so you can see* why *he wrote it . . . I think for a lot of people who don't know about Jim Morrison, it will really help explain a lot. Each song was a real experience he had. It's a great script. It's as near to* No-One Here Gets Out Alive *(Danny Sugerman's book which inspired the movie) as possible.* "

"*I WENT DOWN to where they were shooting one of those scenes where Morrison is breaking-up this New York hotel room. I gotta admit, he did it exactly as I would have done it. So I think Doors fans are going to be knocked out!* "

"*I HEARD THEY played my version of 'L.A. Woman' on KLOS (a local L.A. station), and when the DJ asked people to phone in with their comments, the switchboard lit-up! People were saying they liked it as much as the original, and that I'd sort of made it my own . . .* "

"*I ADMIRED THE Doors because they never pandered to a hard rock stance. They were able to make music that conjured a lot of different cultures. They played the blues, and sometimes they almost made folk music. The thread that linked it all was rock 'n' roll.* "

"*WHEN I FIRST went to work in America, I did wonder what people might see in my singing. It was pretty obvious that I wasn't like Robert Plant or something, and that Jim Morrison, Iggy Pop, John Lennon, Lou Reed and Elvis were more the sort of people that sang the way I liked. And of course when I got to the States, there was a kind of Doors explosion in the early eighties. And it was kind of like, 'Oh, that's where I fit in a little bit more,' because I was singing in that kind of range. I always loved his music, and I always did 'L.A. Woman' live, so it was just a matter of time before I recorded it.* "

"*'L.A. WOMAN' IS a great jam song – especially when I got this new band together. Everybody knew it, and you can just play that riff over and over again. In fact, that song was the inspiration for 'White Wedding' and 'Rebel Yell'. That never-ending beat, that throb, that pulse. I've been into that for a long long time. It was one of the first things we played, and it went down so well – I* had *to put it on the album. The only bit I left out is when Jim chants 'Mojo risin'. No way was I gonna do that. I mean, that's his. It's sacred. It's an anagram of his name and all. So I think I put a bit of us in there with the Johnny Burnette take on 'Wine Spodeeodee' instead.* "

"*EVERYTHING MORRISON DID, he did for artistic reasons – he wasn't on a death trip. There was always a sense of purpose . . . If you're passionate about life, you can't help but be drawn into things one way or another. The* wild *thing about life is that you can be shattered on the rocks of your own existence through the things you fall in love with, because you want to get too much out of them . . . Now, like the bike I'm having built right now. Obviously I'd rather not have accidents. But you've got to do something to hang yourself out there, to experience something that really puts your nose up against the wall of life.*"

"*MY LIVER, IT'S terrible. The doctors have warned me about it quite a few times. But it's quite good because, in America, they have this thing on your licence which says, 'What organ would you donate if you were in a bad accident?' And I always put my liver. Can you imagine? The doctor's running through the hospital with glee saying, 'We got one! We got a liver!' And the other doctor goes, 'Whose is it? Billy* Idol's. *Oh* nooooooo!' *Ha-ha!*"

"*I CAN BE more than just a rebel with a sexy sneer. And I'm a* lot *more than someone who just wiggles his hips a bit and shows off. I've got a reputation for violence and danger, that I just don't deserve.*"

"*AS LONG AS your personal development goes in line with your music, then you can conquer the problem of being the same. I want to show people I'm a growing human being, not some cartoon image they see on MTV.*"

"*PEOPLE WALK AROUND outside my gigs with placards saying, 'Billy Idol Is A Satanist' and, 'Billy Idol Is The Next Anti-Christ', but the songs I write support love and beauty.*"

"*I KNOW THAT people would rather read about how weird and drug-crazed and sex-mad I am, but I'm not – and I'm determined to prove it. I was a rebel, and in some ways I still am, but I'm not 'Idol The Idiot' and I won't let people label me that way.*"

"*THE THING ABOUT writing songs, is that you want to dig into yourself, to have that ability to sing about things other people recognise in their own lives. And the more you can tap into that, it helps your personality to grow to where people look to see if there's something new there.*"

"*I LIKE THE idea that I've sort of created my own niche in a way, and I'm sort of known for it. So that's the best thing really. I write about things that happen to me. I've often thought of writing about things you read in the paper – things that sort of strike you as awful or whatever – but they never really quite come out like the songs I've actually lived. All people kind of go through the same things in life and, one way or another, you're sort of going to touch the same buttons in other people.*"

"*I JUST LIKE to think of my music as, well, rock 'n' roll really. Obviously you can dance to it at home, but I think it's a lot more rock 'n' roll than a lot of what people call rock 'n' roll nowadays. I think that's the point. There's a lot of rock out there, but there's not much roll! I like to think that I've got enough rhythm 'n' blues in there to say that it's rock 'n' roll.*"

"THE WHOLE IDEA of punk rock was to bring out some sort of alternative music to what had gone before. And I just feel that, even though there's a lot of bands around that are really good, or who are having a lot of success at times, really they're just mimicking what's gone before. They're just reproducing things rather than sort of trying to melt things together and trying to go for a different sound – whatever that means. That's why I've kinda stuck to the sound I want, because it really is kinda me. I wanted to have something about me that gave people a choice. If they were like, 'I don't like heavy rock,' at least there's this. It's still got loud guitars and it's still ballsy, but it's just not that bang-clod-bang-clod, that makes you feel like, well – if you bought a record in 1972, you could have got the same thing, y'know . . . "

"ACCORDING TO THE press, I'm either dying of AIDS, and have to have my blood changed regularly in some hush-hush clinic, or I'm actually already dead! They like explosive headlines in America, and something like 'Billy Idol Is Dead', is much better than saying 'He's alive and well and quietly working on his music.' It gives you a bit of a turn though, I can tell you! "

"PEOPLE JUST MAKE of me what they will. Like, I'm riding my motorcycle around L.A. and I have this accident, and people say, 'I expect that's how he'd like to have died.' But the idea of riding a motorcycle isn't to die. *It's to get to the other end! "*

"I CAN'T COMPLAIN. What rock 'n' roll has done for me, is take me on one long global holiday. Wow! Fancy that! It's better than squatting in Bromley. "

"MY SWIMMING POOL'S built like a lagoon, there are loads of palm trees. My house actually once belonged to a soft-porn merchant, which appealed to my warped sense of humour. Funny thing is, I keep spotting my house in movies on the soft-porn movie channel – y'know, those silly murder stories with loads of strippers being killed off. They used my *house! What a gas! "*

"MY DAD WAS my biggest influence – because he hated pop music. I wanted desperately to prove to him that what I wanted to do wasn't worthless, and that I would *amount to something. But we used to have the most almighty rows. Once, we didn't speak to each other for two years! These days things are different. My dad is impressed by what I've done – I'm rediscovering my parents, and they're rediscovering me. "*

"I NEVER THOUGHT when I was 20, that at 35 I'd still be talking about music and riding motorcycles, but as long as it's exciting I'll continue doing it . . . I don't know what my parents' neighbours think. But I've seen them behind the curtains going, 'He's back – what state's he in this time?' I think they're rather surprised I'm still alive. "

"IT'S BEEN SUCH a long time since I played in England, that I can imagine people wondering if it's for real – or if it's just a video they're watching. "

"I STILL HAVEN'T got all the answers, and I have lots of questions. That's the journey 'Charmed Life' takes – although in no way is it a concept record or any shit like that. It's just that I can't go back to being someone who's nasty and frustrated all the time. I'd just gotten a bit lost. I'd become the type of rock star I used to rebel against. "

"*I THINK I'M lucky that, at the age of 35, I've started to rebuild myself and give myself a second chance. Otherwise, I'd be burned out right now. And that would be the worst thing I could do to Billy Idol.*"

"*I LIKE TO believe that I'm under the protection of God. I believe that we're all under the same spirit, or something. I always liked the poems by Dylan Thomas and Wordsworth and people like that, who believed that there was God in everything and things like that . . . But I've got no basis for my beliefs, so I wouldn't go around shouting them at everybody.*"

"*I DON'T SEE myself as a sex symbol – and neither would* anyone *if they could see me when I first get up!*"

"*I THINK I'VE still got a punk rock attitude. You know, I'm not gonna turn over and die because someone doesn't like Billy Idol, or because someone thinks he's stupid . . . Well, you know, fuck you!*"

"*I CAN BE more than just the old Rebel Yell with a sneer who wiggles his hips a bit and then pisses off. I want to show people that I'm not just a rock 'n' roll thing, I'm a human being.*"

"*ROCK 'N' ROLL can be a thing of beauty and* velvetness, *but a lot of people are too fucking stupid to realise that.*"

"*THESE DAYS I really need my fix of PG Tips and Birds Custard. What I do is, I get the pot, and I warm it up properly, and I get the tea cosy and put the tea bags in, and I get the milk, and I wait a certain amount of time and . . .* aaaaaarrhhh*! I can't* stand *people giving me a tea bag!*"

"*MY CHURCH IS still the dirty bookshop. Everybody heard it wrong. I said I was into porn again – not* born *again!*"

"*MY MOTTO IS . . . 'No deadlines, only headlines!'*"

GENERATION X SINGLES

Your Generation/Day By Day
Chrysalis CHS 2165 September 1977

Wild Youth/Wild Dub
Chrysalis CHS 2189 December 1977

Wild Youth/No No No (mispress B-side)
Chrysalis CHS 2189 December 1977

Ready Steady Go/No No No
Chrysalis CHS 2207 March 1978

King Rocker/Gimme Some Truth
Chrysalis CHS 2261 December 1978

King Rocker/Gimme Some Truth
Chrysalis CHS 2261 (four different coloured vinyl editions, red (Idol), pink (James), orange (Derwood) and yellow (Laff) January 1979

Valley Of The Dolls/Shakin' All Over
Chrysalis CHS 2310 (brown vinyl) February 1979

Valley Of The Dolls/Shakin' All Over
Chrysalis CHS 2310 March 1979

Friday's Angels/Trying For Kicks/This Heat
Chrysalis CHS 2330 (pink vinyl) June 1979

Friday's Angels/Trying For Kicks/This Heat
Chrysalis CHS 2330 June 1979

Dancing With Myself/Ugly Rash
(as Gen X from now)
Chrysalis CHS 2444 September 1980

Dancing With Myself/Ugly Dub/Loopy Dub
Chrysalis CHS 12 2444 (12-inch) September 1980

Dancing With Myself/Untouchables/ King Rocker/Rock On
Chrysalis CHS 2488 (clear vinyl) January 1981

Dancing With Myself/Untouchables/ King Rocker/Rock On
Chrysalis CHS 2488 January 1981

Dancing With Myself/Untouchables/ King Rocker/Rock On
Chrysalis CHS 12 2488 (12-inch) January 1981

King Rocker/Valley Of The Dolls
Old Gold Records OG 9693 February 1987

GENERATION X ALBUMS

Generation X
Chrysalis CHR 1169 March 1978

Valley Of The Dolls
Chrysalis CHR 1193 January 1979

Kiss Me Deadly (as Gen X)
Chrysalis CHR 1327 January 1981

Best Of Generation X
Chrysalis CHM 1521 November 1985

Original Generation X
McDonald Bros Records MBC JOCKLP 9 June 1987

Generation X Live
McDonald Bros Records MBC JOCKLP 11 June 1988

GENERATION X CDs

Generation X
Chrysalis CCD 1169 January 1986

Valley Of The Dolls
Chrysalis CCD 1193 January 1986

Kiss Me Deadly
Chrysalis CCD 1327 January 1986

BILLY IDOL SINGLES

Mony Mony/Baby Talk
Chrysalis CHS 2543 September 1981

Mony Mony/Baby Talk/Untouchables/ Dancing With Myself
Chrysalis CHS 12 2543 (12-inch) September 1981

Hot In The City/Dead On Arrival
Chrysalis CHS 2625 August 1982

Hot In The City/Dead On Arrival
Chrysalis CHS 2625 (picture disc) August 1982

Hot In The City (Extended)/Dead On Arrival
Chrysalis CHS 12 2625 (12-inch) August 1982

White Wedding/Hole In The Wall
Chrysalis CHS 2656 October 1982

White Wedding/Hole In The Wall
Chrysalis CHS 12 2656 (12-inch) October 1982

White Wedding/Hot In The City
Chrysalis IDOL 1 September 1983

White Wedding/Hot In The City
Chrysalis IDOL 1 (clear vinyl) September 1983

White Wedding/Hot In The City/ Dancing With Myself/Love Calling
Chrysalis IDOLX 1 (12-inch) September 1983

Rebel Yell/Crank Call
Chrysalis IDOL 2 January 1984

Rebel Yell/Crank Call/White Wedding
Chrysalis IDOLX 2 (12-inch) January 1984

Rebel Yell/Crank Call/White Wedding
Chrysalis IDOLP 2 (square picture disc) January 1984

Rebel Yell/Crank Call/White Wedding/ Hot In The City
Chrysalis IDOLD 2 (double-pack with gatefold sleeve) January 1984

Eyes Without A Face/The Dead Next Door
Chrysalis IDOL 3 June 1984

Eyes Without A Face/The Dead Next Door
Chrysalis IDOL 3 (gatefold sleeve) June 1984

Eyes Without A Face/The Dead Next Door/ Dancing With Myself/ Rebel Yell
Chrysalis IDOLX 3 (12-inch) June 1984

Eyes Without A Face/The Dead Next Door/ Dancing With Myself/ Rebel Yell
Chrysalis IDOLP 3 (12-inch picture disc) June 1984

Eyes Without A Face/The Dead Next Door/ Dancing With Myself/ Rebel Yell
Chrysalis IDOLD 3 (double-pack) June 1984

Flesh For Fantasy/Blue Highway
Chrysalis IDOL 4 September 1984

Flesh For Fantasy/Blue Highway
Chrysalis IDOL 4 (gatefold sleeve) September 1984

Flesh For Fantasy (Extended)/Blue Highway/ Flesh For Fantasy
Chrysalis IDOLX 4 (12-inch with poster) September 1984

Flesh For Fantasy (Extended)/Blue Highway/ Flesh For Fantasy
Chrysalis IDOLP 4 (12-inch picture disc) September 1984

White Wedding/Flesh For Fantasy
Chrysalis IDOL 5 June 1985

White Wedding/Flesh For Fantasy
Chrysalis IDOL 5 (white vinyl) June 1985

White Wedding (Shotgun Mix, Pts 1&2)/ Mega-Idol-Mix
Chrysalis IDOL 5 June 1985

White Wedding (Shotgun Mix Pts 1&2)/ Mega-Idol-Mix
Chrysalis IDOL 5 (PVC sleeve clear vinyl) June 1985

White Wedding (Shotgun Mix Pts 1&2)/ Mega-Idol-Mix
Chrysalis IDOLX 5 (12-inch) June 1985

White Wedding (Shotgun Mix Pts 1&2)/ Mega-Idol-Mix
Chrysalis IDOLX 5 (12-inch white vinyl) June 1985

White Wedding (Shotgun Mix Pts 1&2)/ Mega-Idol-Mix
Chrysalis IDOLP 5 (12-inch picture disc) June 1985

Rebel Yell/Stand In The Shadows (Live)
Chrysalis IDOL 6 September 1985

Rebel Yell/Stand In The Shadows (Live)
Chrysalis IDOL 6 (gatefold sleeve) September 1985

Rebel Yell/Stand In The Shadows (Live)
Chrysalis IDOL 6 (picture disc) September 1985

Rebel Yell/Stand In The Shadows (Live)/ Blue Highway (Live)
Chrysalis IDOLX 6 (12-inch) September 1985

Rebel Yell/Stand In The Shadows (Live)/ Blue Highway (Live)
Chrysalis IDOLP 6 (12-inch picture disc) September 1985

To Be A Lover/All Summer Single
Chrysalis IDOL 8 September 1986

To Be A Lover/All Summer Single
Chrysalis IDOL 8 (coloured vinyl) September 1986

To Be A Lover (Mercy Mix)/To Be A Lover/ All Summer Single
Chrysalis IDOLX 8 (12-inch) September 1986

To Be A Lover (Mercy Mix)/To Be A Lover/ All Summer Single
Chrysalis IDOLP 8 (12-inch picture disc) September 1986

To Be A Lover/All Summer Single/ White Wedding/Mega-Idol-Mix
Chrysalis IDOLD 8 (double-pack) September 1986

Don't Need A Gun/Fatal Charm
Chrysalis IDOL 9 February 1987

Don't Need A Gun/Fatal Charm
Chrysalis IDOL 9 (coloured vinyl) February 1987

Don't Need A Gun/Fatal Charm
Chrysalis IDOLG 9 (gatefold sleeve) February 1987

Don't Need A Gun (Melt-Down Mix)/ (A Cappella)/Fatal Charm
Chrysalis IDOLP 9 (12-inch picture disc) February 1987

Don't Need A Gun/Fatal Charm/To Be A Lover/ All Summer Single
Chrysalis IDOLD 9 (double-pack) February 1987

Don't Need A Gun (Beyond The Melt-Down Mix)/(Dub Version)/Fatal Charm
Chrysalis IDOLR 9 (12-inch) February 1987

Sweet Sixteen/Beyond Belief
Chrysalis IDOL 10 May 1987

Sweet Sixteen/Beyond Belief/Rebel Yell
Chrysalis IDOLX 10 (12-inch) May 1987

Sweet Sixteen/Beyond Belief/Rebel Yell
Chrysalis IDOLP 10 (12-inch picture disc) May 1987

Mony Mony/Shakin' All Over (Live)
Chrysalis IDOL 11 October 1987

Mony Mony (Hung Like A Pony Mix)/ Shakin' All Over (Live)/Mony Mony (Live)
Chrysalis IDOLX 11 (12-inch) October 1987

Hot In The City (Remix)/Catch My Fall (Remix)
Chrysalis IDOL 12 January 1988

Hot In The City (Exterminator Mix)/ Catch My Fall (Remix)/Soul Standing By
Chrysalis IDOLX 12 (12-inch) January 1988

Hot In The City (Exterminator Mix)/ Catch My Fall (Remix)/Soul Standing By
Chrysalis IDOLP 12 (12-inch picture disc) January 1988

Hot In The City (Exterminator Mix)/Catch My Fall/Soul Standing By/Mony Mony
Chrysalis IDOLCD 12 (CD) January 1988

Catch My Fall/All Summer Single
Chrysalis IDOL 13 August 1988

Catch My Fall/All Summer Single
Chrysalis IDOLX 13 (12-inch) August 1988

Catch My Fall/All Summer Single
Chrysalis IDOLCD 13 (CD) August 1988

Catch My Fall/All Summer Single
Chrysalis IDOLB 13 (limited edition box set with badge and personality card) August 1988

Cradle Of Love/311 Man
Chrysalis IDOL 14 April 1990

Cradle Of Love (Extended Mix)/(LP Version)/ Rob The Cradle Of Dub (Extended Mix)
Chrysalis IDOLX 14 (12-inch) April 1990

Cradle Of Love (Edit)/(Extended Mix)/ (LP Version)/Rob The Cradle Of Dub (Extended Mix)/311 Man
Chrysalis IDOLCD 14 (CD) April 1990

Cradle Of Love/311 Man
Chrysalis IDOLMC 14 (cassette) April 1990

Cradle Of Dub (Extended Mix)/Cradle Of Love (LP Version)/ Rob The Cradle Of Dub (Extended Mix)/311 Man
Chrysalis IDOLXP 14 (12-inch picture disc) April 1990

L.A. Woman/License To Thrill
Chrysalis IDOL 15 August 1990

L.A. Woman (LP Version)/License To Thrill/ Lovechild
Chrysalis IDOLX 15 (12-inch) August 1990

L.A. Woman/License To Thrill/Lovechild
Chrysalis IDOLCD 15 (CD) August 1990

L.A. Woman/License To Thrill
Chrysalis IDOLMC 15 (cassette) August 1990

L.A. Woman (LP Version)/License To Thrill/ Lovechild
Chrysalis IDOLXP 15 (12-inch picture disc) August 1990

BILLY IDOL ALBUMS

Billy Idol
Chrysalis CHR 1377 July 1982

Rebel Yell
Chrysalis CHR 1450 January 1984

Vital Idol
Chrysalis CUX 1502 June 1985

Whiplash Smile
Chrysalis CDL 1514 October 1986

An Interview With Billy Idol
Lip Service LSM 02 November 1986

Interview Picture Disc
Music And Media IDOL 1001 February 1988

Idol Songs – 11 Of The Best
Chrysalis BIL TV 1 (first 50,000 include an additional picture disc LP, featuring six 12-inch remixes) June 1988

Interview Picture Disc
Baktabak BAK 2103 August 1988

Charmed Life
Chrysalis CHR 1735 April 1990

BILLY IDOL CDs

Billy Idol
Chrysalis ACCD 1377 January 1986

Rebel Yell
Chrysalis ACCD 1450 January 1986

Vital Idol
Chrysalis CCD 1502 January 1986

Whiplash Smile
Chrysalis CCD 1514 October 1986

Idol Songs – 11 Of The Best
Chrysalis BIL CD 1 (with additional extended mixes of 'Eyes Without A Face', 'To Be A Lover', 'Don't Need A Gun' and 'Mony Mony') June 1988

Charmed Life
Chrysalis CCD 1735 April 1990